OUT OF ORDER

MY LIFE - WITH PARKINSON'S

BY

RAY WEGRZYN

-oOo-

Acknowledgements.

I learnt long ago that lists can be dangerous things, especially ones that are being made public. A list is deliberate. It may be prepared at very short notice or be considered over days. But either way, it is deliberate. And almost inevitably, there will be items missed. Not a problem if talking about the grocery list. But a list of people that has attempted to be fully inclusive of some category or another, which misses out anyone who is viewed as belonging to that category and you cause pain. No matter how well a missed off person deals with their absence from the list, there is a feeling of some degree of rejection. So I rarely make lists of people any more. The people in my life who have made any sort of contribution to the story in this book will know who they are even if they do not know the impact they have had. I hope that they realise how much I appreciate them.

The following people have, in addition to anything else, made a significant practical contribution to the production of this book.

Allan Amato for Cover photograph
Stephen Hubbard for early draft edit and encouragement
Paul Muszanskyj for advice, book cover design and layout.
Wasyl Muszanskyj for commentary and support
Richard Wegrzyn for a thorough final edit.

Above all,
this is for Dot, Matthew and Danielle and Richard and Jen
because they are here for me
whatever is to come.

Foreword.

When Ray asked me to write a foreword to his book I agreed instantly. Not because I was flattered but because I have known him all of my life and I wanted the opportunity to say it as it is. Not gushing or romanticized but simply a reflection of who he is.

Ray has Parkinson's. He doesn't suffer from it, he deals with it positively, realistically and adapts and then he gets on with his life.

If there is one impression that you glean after reading his account, I believe that it will be that of an inspirational, loyal person who lives life to the full. An individual who has a wonderful, loving family and numerous friends, not all of whom he has mentioned but all of whom are greatly appreciated. Someone who is actively engaged and instrumental in improving other peoples' lives. A man who happens to have Parkinson's.

Parkinson's doesn't define him. It is just another aspect of what is an otherwise rich and fulfilled life.

His account of his life (so far) is sometimes funny, sometimes tragic and always positive despite life's challenges.

I hope you gain as much as I did from reading it, as, despite the fact that I have known him since infancy, there is always something to be learnt about those closest to you.

Wasyl Muszanskyj

Contents

Chapter 1 - Disjointed

He snarled at me. His breath stank and spittle frothed around the corners of his mouth. His eyes were bulging with the force of his anger and I'm absolutely sure that if his teeth got anywhere near me they would have ripped chunks out. I had hold of his collars in both hands. My hands were crossed over which meant that when I pulled my right hand his right side came forward. This gave me better control over his balance and thus better control of him, although I had to admit that I was getting a bit worried about the situation.

Despite the excellent grip I had on his collars I didn't have full control of his arms and he kept trying to whack me, left and right. I was able to use my elbows as blocks. I had taken a moderately deep stance to give me a stable base. This meant that although I was lower than him he had to lean forward to try to hit me, so destabilising his own stance. If I needed to, I could put him down, but I didn't really fancy scrabbling on the floor if it could be avoided.

He was regularly attempting to kick me on the shin or in the balls. Again, my stance was helpful, in that I could pivot sideways as well as move quickly backwards to avoid these efforts. The hard part now was trying to keep an eye on everything and make sure I avoided his feet without ever letting go of him or overstepping the line in terms of how much I hurt him. The law isn't always automatically on the side of the good guy.

It had been a simple enough stop. I was walking through the supermarket car park, heading inside to pick up a few basics for the fridge freezer before it became completely empty and forgot how to chill food. I heard, rather than saw, a commotion and a woman's voice shout "stop him, he's got my bag". I turned in the direction of the sound to see a dishevelled looking man in his late 20s, with lank, greasy hair. He was clutching an elegant red leather handbag and he was running hard in my direction.

I stood my ground and could tell from the look on his face that he expected me to shift. I turned 45 degrees, slightly bent my knees and brought my left hand up in the universally recognised 'Stop' sign. He yelled at me "get out of the fucking way". I looked him straight in the eye and waited. There was a huge, windowless brick wall to my left, probably the side of the warehouse part of the superstore and a variety of cars parked on my right. Finally, I saw the first sign of hesitation as he tried to decide which way to go around me. I wanted him against the wall so I stepped to my right to make the gap between myself and the cars narrower. He accelerated and went towards the wall clearly wanting to slip by me and get away rather than to deal with the confrontation, given that despite being only 5' 8" I wasn't moving out of his way. I counted the moments and waited to the last millisecond before doing two quick sidesteps to my left. By now he was running more or less against the wall and could not move out to my right and get away from me. He decided that sheer force was the answer and accelerated towards the narrowing gap between my left shoulder and the wall. I braced myself waiting for the inevitable clash, knowing that he would put the brakes on at the last moment which would take a lot of the steam out of his run. I in return would not ease up on my brace one iota, so leaving him to run relatively slowly and without drive into an immovable object angled out deliberately to stop him. The plan worked as I knew it would and although I certainly felt the blow I was ready for it and he was not. I turned with him, reaching out to grab his collars which allowed me to put him in a throttle position against the wall if I needed to. Thus we come to the current situation. I have to wait for people to organise themselves to call the cops. I don't want to, I want to get my shopping and go home. I shout "I've got him". And hope that people will react reasonably quickly.

It was at this point that he overstepped the mark. He spat straight in my face. I nutted him, without thinking. It was an automatic response and a perfect Manchester kiss. At the same time my right knee rammed into his groin. His eyes went up in his head and he dropped into a deadweight on the floor. I let go as he was halfway down. I was very sorry that his head bounced on the concrete again.

I picked up the red leather handbag, turned and started to walk towards the gathering crowd, hand up and palm forward so no-one would mistake me for the bad guy. Suddenly I heard the revving engine and I turned again just in time to see the car heading straight towards me. I leapt...

...it was dark. Something hard was sticking into my back and I was surrounded by a soft fabric. I seemed to be tied in a knot. I tried to move but found that my arms were underneath my body. Very slowly, realisation came. I was in my bedroom. I had gone to bed and that was the last thing I remember... no, apart from dealing with the robbery in the supermarket car park I think and then the car coming... Now, I wasn't in a supermarket car park I was in my bedroom. Yes. That's it. So, why am I wrapped in fabric? I wriggled around until I could free my arms and I used them to liberate myself from the cocoon of quilt. It was quite dark and I gently felt around me. As I was doing this I began to feel the pain in the middle of my forehead. I could feel that my nails were bent on several fingers. Finally my flapping hands came in contact with what I worked out to be my bed. From this I oriented myself and climbed back on it. My right knee was hurting as well now and after a minute or two I reached up and switched on the light. Blinking, I looked around me. The bed was a mess and a number of items had fallen off the cupboard across the room. Two of my nails were completely broken and another couple were bent back. I looked down at my right knee which was sore and very red. Finally, I got out of the bed and hobbled out of my room to a mirror on the landing. My forehead was beginning to show a bruise right in the middle.

"Dammit" I thought "another fine example of Parkinson's screwing me over." Active Rapid Eye Movement (REM) sleep strikes again. Normally when asleep, physical movement is separated from thought, allowing us to have lively dreams without moving very much at all in our beds. A number of people suffer from a condition known as active REM sleep. This is more prevalent in people with Parkinson's than in the general population. Effectively it means that you act out what you dream. So yes, in my mind I had needed to stop a robber. I had to use force to do so and then violence in reaction to his assault and finally had to leap out of the way of a vehicle. In reality I had lain in my bed, assaulted the wall, hurt myself and eventually leapt out, crashing into the cupboard across the room. And it had all happened in a very few moments, whilst I was unconscious.

This was about the fifth time in ten or so years that this had happened in such a dramatic manner. The first two times were in that period of married life when we shared a bed. Unfortunately, although I had not dreamt about assaulting her, Dot, my long suffering wife of some 34 years, was there and of course and in the way of my flailing fists. She came off the worst in the encounter and was too frightened to have me in the bed anymore. I couldn't blame her and since the boys had left we had a spare room, so we agreed that I would move into it. It's not the best arrangement for married life, but it allows her to get some sleep and me to wander around in the middle of the night when I can't. Conjugal activity is relatively easily addressed, although truth be told I miss the company. Just one of the many wedges that Parkinson's disease can drive between couples. Yes, how people handle it makes all the difference but what a shame people have to address such challenges. When I was originally told I had Parkinson's at the age of 39 in July 1995, I expected I would have to deal with a tremor and slowing down. I had no idea of the full impact it would have.

So, that's what this story is about. One man's journey through a life affected by Parkinson's. An exploration of what made me respond as I have done. I hope you might find it half as interesting to read as I have to live.

Chapter 2 – Found Out

By training I'm a probation officer. I'm married to Dot, who I met when we both worked at the Cambrian Unit in Manchester, a special educational unit for severely mentally disturbed children. We have two lovely, bright, caring boys, Matthew and Richard. We should also have had Conrad, but more about him later. We have made our home in Glossop, Derbyshire, a pleasant town just at the foot of the Pennines before the Snake Pass over to Sheffield from Manchester. We moved there in September 1981 when Matthew was about six weeks old and I was about to start my probation officer training at Manchester Polytechnic. The boys are both married now and living independently, gainfully employed and both, as far as I can tell, happy in their circumstances. They are both married to girls we are proud to have as our daughters-in-law. Diligent, well brought up and sensible without being stuffy.

Our lives have been, in many ways, straightforward. Like so many people, there have been a few crises and catastrophes, but overall more happiness than sadness and more progress than fallings down.

I guess the thing that has had the biggest effect in the sense of its long-term presence and its increasing impact was my diagnosis with Parkinson's disease. I hate to admit that. I hate having it. At the time of writing, I am 21 years post diagnosis. (I was a few weeks off my fortieth birthday at that time). I have been retired since late 2011 because of it. We moved house in November 2013, having lived in our first Glossop home for 30 years and only moving because of a chance opportunity to live in a lovely dormer bungalow on the side of a steep hill with beautiful views over the Peak District.

I'm still considered to be young to have had this particular condition (I don't use the word disease alongside Parkinson's. It's not contagious, it doesn't follow the same path for everybody and people are not classically ill as they would tend to be considered to be in the clutches of a disease) for such a length of time. In some ways I feel like a veteran, in others I'm an absolute rookie. I'm a veteran because I have been fencing with this thing for such a long time. I have learned to accept the daily or even hourly variation in how I feel and how gross or mild my symptoms might be irrespective of how accurate or otherwise I am in terms of timing my medication. I've come to accept that I can't do certain things even if my head tells me that I probably could manage, my body quickly says "don't believe that!" I have come to recognise that the fatigue which Parkinson's brings is added to by the medication I take and more than that, it is not like the fatigue that comes with a few nights without sleep. It is hard to describe but as you read through the book you'll see that I try to make it accessible. I'm a rookie because it continues to throw new challenges in front of my feet which it has already hobbled because, I think, it just enjoys watching the struggle. Am I anthropomorphising? You bet your bottom dollar. If I see it as a human I can imagine the fight. If I see it as a surreal, cloud-like concept, fighting it gets very difficult. So when it suits me and because I can do as I please as far as that is concerned, I view Parkinson's as if I am facing a man who intends to hurt me and I intend not to let him.

I'm not, in fact, a violent man. I have had fights on three occasions in my life (each of which I'm relieved to say I won) and been beaten up twice. It all happened in my early teens and I'm pleased to say the beatings happened first, and the three wins happened subsequently. I've never had a fight as an adult and hope I never do because I would be hopeless now. Hopeless not because I have lost my fighting spirit, far from it but simply because the net effect of Parkinson's over the years saps your strength and speed of reaction. So in my head I am a warrior and my perspective on my situation is that I am at war with Parkinson's. I hope that this will unfold and become clearer and perhaps more understandable as you read on.

I learned through these events that I am no observer of the Queensbury rules. Outside of sport in the ring, there is no such thing as a fair fight. There is only winning or losing. When it matters and you're the one who may win or lose then there is no point trying for anything other than a complete victory. The three opponents I fought in my teenage years had each pushed me into a corner, no doubt with certain expectations about my reactions. In fact, each of them went away hurt. They had not expected me to be able to do that and I knew that that was the only thing that was going to leave me intact. Sometimes it's no bad thing to exceed expectations. I also learned that sometimes you have to look after yourself even if the cost is one of losing a friend. It's knowing when that is the situation one is in that is the difficult part. These lessons served me well throughout my adult life and no doubt contributed to the way that I have chosen to deal with having a chronic degenerative neurological disorder for which there is no cure.

I was born in August 1955 and raised in central Manchester. I went to St Joseph's primary school on Plymouth Grove and to Xaverian college grammar school. I grew up with my mum, my older brother Paul and my younger sister Sheila and I'll explain a lot more about those early years further on.

I started working for the Probation Service in Greater Manchester when I was 19 years old, as a sessional worker on the then brand-new community service scheme. At the time, I was working full-time Monday to Friday at a special unit for severely autistic children. Dot also worked there and between us we had very little in the way of income. A friend of mine who worked for the probation service suggested I might consider a part-time role which would also add to my weekly income. Accordingly, after being appointed, I would turn up on a Saturday or Sunday outside the office in Minshull Street in the centre of Manchester to collect four or five adults who had been made subject to a court order as an alternative to custody. Instead, they were required to do unpaid work of benefit to the community. It was my job to see that they did it as required. I suppose one way of doing work like that is to do it along the lines of the American warden overseeing the chain gang. Tell people what to do and then watch them do it and chastise them if they get it wrong. Another way of doing it is to engage with people, help them to figure out how to do things that they can't do, and have a rather better day whilst doing it. I chose the latter and after a year found that I had some affinity with the idea of people changing their attitudes and behaviour. The men that I had met (because they were overwhelmingly male offenders) were a very mixed bag both in terms of age, current circumstances and experience of life.

What they had in common though was a degree of inadequacy, an inability to assess a risk and see potential pitfalls and the ability to convince themselves that they couldn't get caught. What I found I had was the ability to talk about these things with people, challenge their perceptions and point out to them other ways of achieving things. I'm not going to pretend to you that that's the be all and end all of being a probation officer but as a starting point at that time it wasn't bad.

When a vacancy came up as an unqualified officer full-time on the community service team, responsible for a caseload of offenders, assessing, placing them at work, overseeing their progress and enforcing the order should they fail to comply, I decided to have a go. I completed my first formal application form, was invited for an interview, turned up and answered the questions I was asked the best way I knew how and to my amazement was offered the post. So at 21 although I didn't know it at that time, I started working my way up a career ladder which was to be a not unreasonable one.

I think we are a fairly orthodox family. My wife Dot, myself and two boys Matthew and Richard, have lived in a small stone cottage in Glossop in Derbyshire since December 1984. At the time that I'm writing about, the boys were around 13 and 12. There's a little one missing. Conrad would have been with us had he not died during his birth in 1989. Had that not happened, we would have been living in Cambridgeshire. I had secured a post as Senior Probation Officer down there just before he was due and we had a plan for me to go and find a place to live whilst Dot stayed in Glossop with the children. We would then all move down to Cambridge and make a life there. When Conrad died, during my period of notice, I couldn't cope with leaving my family or indeed being on my own down there and so I withdrew from the post and remained working as a main grade probation officer in Salford. Happily for me it wasn't long before I was given the post as an acting senior in Oldham which I secured three months later as a permanent promotion. Our family was quite traditional in the sense that I went out to work and Dot stayed home, working part time as a child minder and latterly as a crèche worker, raising the children. We were both pretty good at what we did and from our point of view, our arrangement worked well.

The detail behind most of this will unfold throughout this story and I don't intend to pack it all in here. Suffice to say that my life went along reasonably happily and reasonably normally through working as a community service officer, going off to train as a probation officer between 1981 and 83, becoming a father, qualifying as a probation officer and starting work in Salford, a borough with a reputation of high crime and poverty. Over the next decade between 1988 and 1998 I became a bereaved parent, a senior probation officer, a project worker for the Home Office on a national information system implementation and a person living with Parkinson's. This is how that last role started.

At a point in time post 1989, but one that I can't precisely pinpoint, I became aware of a tiny tic occurring periodically in my left arm, just at the top left hand side of my bicep. It wasn't troublesome at all, simply a slight distraction when it occurred. It wasn't the sort of thing worth going to the doctor about. It didn't hurt. It didn't cause any consequential difficulty that I was aware of. It was just a tic. Except that two or three years later, I was a little taken aback when my friend Richard called around for a coffee and a chat as usual. Apropos of nothing he said "you know you've got that tic in your arm don't you?" I looked at him and made some dismissive noise at which point we both laughed. I made us both a brew and we sat talking as we so often did about everything and nothing.

Almost at the end of the visit, the subject got back to the tic in my arm. Richard mentioned it again and I replied "it's nothing" "it's been there for years."
"It's got worse in the time I've been watching it" Richard told me.
"Why haven't you mentioned it before?"
"Well, you know..." he muttered.
I grunted in a manly way.

I thought about that conversation a lot for a couple of weeks and then had to admit some truths to myself. The first of these was that it had got worse. The second one was that I had no idea what had started it; the third truth was that I had no idea what it was. I knew I needed to go to the doctor's, but at that time I had no idea of the rollercoaster journey that the visit would kick off.

I was, by now, aware that the tic had expanded into a slight tremor in my left arm. It wasn't particularly bad, it didn't particularly bother me, but it clearly wasn't right. I mentioned it to Dot, who gave me the fully expected, sensible advice; "you best get to the doctor then".

As is usual for me, I had looked up 'tremor' as a symptom in several medical books. I enjoy research and learning things in an informal way. All of the books I looked at identified Parkinson's or Multiple Sclerosis as the key conditions for which tremor would be an indicative symptom. I had read up on both of these. If you had to have one of them it would be better to have Parkinson's I decided. I had initially believed that this was based on an objective assessment of the two conditions, but it was purely a gut reaction to what seemed to be a shorter, more intense and ultimately sometimes fatal condition of MS compared to a longer, drawn-out experience of Parkinson's which could be relatively mild. Dreams are wonderful things aren't they?

I duly made an appointment to see my GP who I had known for several years. He was a perfectly pleasant man, perhaps a little distant and inattentive sometimes but better that than somebody who was dismissive. This would have been around March of 1993. As I started to tell him why I was there I was shocked that the tremor kicked in more aggressively than it had ever done before, not only in my arm where it had always existed but also my left leg and foot which I had not noticed tremoring previously. This was positive in terms of being able to show him what I was talking about but alarming to me as to why talking to the doctor should generate such a reaction.
"How long has it been like that?"
I explained that I couldn't remember exactly when I had first noticed it and then briefly told him the story of Richard's challenge to me.
"Any pain?" he asked and then almost immediately "does that tic happen anywhere else?"
He made some notes and then turned to me and said:

"It's probably nothing serious. It could be a thyroid problem. We'll take a blood test and see what that tells us."

So I was out of the starting gate heading down the front straight with no idea whatsoever of how long it would be before I had an actual diagnosis and received any treatment at all. It's enormously difficult to pace yourself for a race that has no identifiable end. So, I made an appointment to have blood tests taken. The results came back as normal which I was told two weeks later when I went back to see the GP. He said that he wanted to refer me to a neurologist at the local hospital for him to form an opinion. When I asked him what that might be, he fudged and gave a very general answer. I said it was fine and he should go ahead and make the referral as there was clearly something to be identified and hopefully sorted out. I can recall wondering if he knew more than he was telling me and deciding that he probably did because after all he's a doctor. He's familiar with how bad things start off as small things. For my part I had moved a step nearer to knowing, albeit at that stage I still genuinely didn't know what might be going on.

Moving slowly, as these things are wont to do, it was several weeks before the appointment letter arrived suggesting a date and time for me to attend the blue outpatients area, which date was once again at least a couple of months hence. I was blessed with a busy job and family life which kept my mind well occupied and focused on immediate issues. This is a terribly useful distraction for any worry that I might get into about my health. Worrying comes naturally to me. It is spurred on by my lapsed Catholicism and my absolute conviction that I'm responsible for everything bad that happens. So I avoided thinking too much about anything to do with my health, preferring instead to take responsibility for the Spanish Inquisition, until the day before I was due to attend to meet the neurologist. I didn't suffer a particularly high level of stress at that point, probably because I didn't know what might be involved. I was worried, so I kept it to myself as that is usually the best place for those things.

The day of the appointment duly dawned and I got up, showered and breakfasted. I put on my suit and polished my shoes thinking that somehow, if I was well turned out, things might not be as bad as if I went in jeans and a T-shirt. The drive to the hospital was very familiar to me, one that I'd done many times as a result of working as a social worker in the same catchment area years before and of the children needing to attend for this, that and the other. I parked up and walked across to the new part of the hospital where the outpatients unit is based. Once I arrived in the right area it was an easy matter to find the blue section as it was painted blue. I stood for a few minutes until a seat became free on the patient's side of the Plexiglas windows. The receptionist was brisk and efficient and carefully sealed the envelope containing my documents about me before she handed them to me and invited me to go to the blue waiting area. I followed the corridor for a few metres watching for signs for the blue waiting area. Once I got there, (there were no signs, just blue walls) a nurse immediately relieved me of the envelope, no doubt fearing I might actually look at what was written about me and gently directed "take a seat for me".

One of life's pet irritants is the habit some people have, of inviting you, perhaps in a hospital or doctor's surgery or an office for a meeting with somebody to "take a seat for me".

21

When I have arrived somewhere for a visit, whether by appointment or not, I'm planning to stay until I've done my business with them. I'm quite happy to sit down and wait. But I don't see why I should do that 'for them'. I'd rather do it for myself. There are a number of situations where this type of phrase is used excessively and because I've noticed it and find it rather irritating I do hear it loud and clear every time it's used.

Now of course I know that this is not something people are saying consciously. It's a little pat delivery which trips off the tongue, probably without the person saying it even being aware of what they're saying. They might as well be pressing a button for a sign as speaking to me thoughtfully. It honestly causes me no problem, it just slightly grates every time It's said to me, which is quite often.

Having raised this issue, I do want to make it clear that I'm not judging or casting aspersions on the people who say these things. They're probably saying them dozens of times a day and like everybody in work we all have our little personal routines that get us through the day. Of course it would be a wonderful world if everybody could stand in another person's shoes and experience life from that perspective. This would have many implications, some of which would be very important and others of which, like not saying "take a seat for me" would be just a tiny bit of tidying up "for me."

I sat quietly waiting to be called after the usual kerfuffle in pronouncing my surname. Once I had fenced with the receptionist and the clinic nurse about pronunciation, I was called in to the consultant's lair, where my whole future was to be ripped open and redesigned. First though, the inevitable conversation about the pronunciation of my surname.

I am ridiculously proud of my ridiculous surname. There are a number of reasons for that, several of which will become clear later on. The name is Polish. It is not a common Polish name and although now much more widespread, 20 years ago and prior to that it was really only found in a very small part of the sub-Carpathian region in the south east of Poland. My father comes from a village called Miejsce Piestowe. The word 'Wegrzyn' probably means Hungarian. We think it likely that either a village moved or a boundary was moved and a group of people from Hungary became a group of people in Poland. They most probably stuck together and would have been referred to by others as the Hungarians. This then would have become the surname of anyone who lived in the village. Visits to the village cemetery made by my sister when she was 18 identified many gravestones with the name Wegrzyn engraved on them, but most were not our relatives.

The actual pronunciation requires the inclusion of a Polish E. Their alphabet has several versions of E, one of which has a small hook underneath rather like a French cedilla. That hook makes the E into an EN sound. In Polish of course, W is pronounced as a V and so we have the word 'Wegrzyn' pronounced as 'Vengjen'. Or at least this is as near as English can get to the correct pronunciation. I never tire of helping people pronounce and learn to spell it and doubt that I ever will.

Chapter 3 –Initial Engagement

The consulting chamber that we were sitting in was uniformly grey/beige, slightly grubby, with institutional furniture. Functional, but not particularly comfortable. Although there was a large window, I could not see out of it because of the patterned glass and the window blind. I so wanted to be able to look out and have a view of the hills of the dark peak which bring me such comfort every time I come home from one of my work trips. I don't know if you have ever had the joy of living from a suitcase. Hotel rooms have a certain cachet, a certain attraction when you start using them regularly. The longer that goes on the more shine comes off the lifestyle. When I started travelling significantly for work, in 2002, I can remember being quite anxious and needing to know some time in advance where I was going to be, when and how I was going to get there. After a few years of increasing time away, I was now a seasoned traveller who could receive a phone call in the morning and be anywhere in the country at the end of the day, ready to hit the place to be inspected first thing the following morning. And there's a weariness that comes with it. Travelling home becomes the highlight of the week. It may be the highlight of the day when one commutes, in which case a person is lucky to have five highlights of the week but I suspect it becomes more mundane, more routine the more often it occurs. Setting off on Sunday and arriving back on Friday gives you plenty of time to miss that which you have chosen to enjoy. That can apply to the locality as much as it might apply to one's family and friends.

The doctor was getting on in years. He was really quite an unprepossessing man. Mind you, saying that, I'm not sure what image I had for a consultant neurologist. I suppose a typical mad professor type with stethoscope round his neck and a pickled brain on his desk. He had grey, curly hair, was about my height and had a less than brilliant personal manner for dealing with people whom he must surely have realised were at best a little anxious and at worst worried sick. He had taken some details from me and asked me various questions and conducted the usual examinations, listening to the heart and chest etc. He then conducted a peculiar series of exercises; he asked me to tap my left hand on my thigh. Then he started to clap. I was completely taken aback. When I was slapping my thigh whilst he was clapping, I was hitting on the beat. As soon as he stopped clapping and asked me to move the fingers on my right hand my left hand went completely off rhythm. He then asked me to touch each finger of each hand to its thumb in order and again doing that to his count was fine. As soon as there was a distraction by doing a different activity with the other side of my body I lost the rhythm. These are not the sort of things that one does at home or that anybody asks you to do and so it was a completely new experience for me to find that my body didn't work the way that I would have expected it to.

Having done all these assessments, and whilst I was fastening my shirt, he muttered more to himself it seemed than to me "well it looks like you've got Parkinson's disease, but you're far too young."
There. He had said The Words. The statement that I longed to hear and was desperately afraid of hearing. I had no idea how to react. I waited for the next comment. "I want you to see somebody else. Can you get to London?"

I said "I'm down there every week with work so I guess it's not a problem".

"Okay" he said, "let's get a CAT scan done just to rule out anything else. If that's clear I might sort an MRI scan for you, and then I'd like to get you an appointment at the National Neurological Hospital in London to see Dr Niall Quinn, who is a leading specialist in Parkinson's Disease, so we can get his opinion." And so I was dismissed.

I walked back to the car and got in for the half hour drive home, wondering how I felt. I had arrived at the hospital knowing that if I had to have something wrong I wanted it to be Parkinson's disease rather than multiple sclerosis, which was the alternative, as far as I was concerned. Having been sort of given the news that I "wanted" I realised that I would rather not have any of it. I had done a reasonable amount of research into tremor as a symptom. Having identified Parkinson's and MS as the most likely conditions, I also knew from that research that I was not too young to have Parkinson's disease and was surprised at hearing the neurologist make that comment. Indeed I was at the upper end of the age range for developing MS which also made Parkinson's disease a more likely diagnosis in my mind. So despite having now been assessed by a specialist and having heard the words from a professional for the first time I was still not clear what the situation was and therefore what its implications were.

I drove home with a fuzzy head that couldn't really process anything beyond the simple facts of what happened and what had been said. Not a position I like to find myself in. I felt flat. Not relieved, of course, because that would only have been brought about by somebody saying categorically that there was nothing the matter with me. Not upset, because I didn't know what I had, albeit that suspicions were raised and perhaps a particular path was now being trod. Just flat. There was little to tell when I got home apart from a straightforward account of what happened. I needed to wait for the next steps or the ones after that or indeed the ones after that, before I would finally know what it was that I was facing.

Chapter 4 – A Testing Time

Four days later an envelope came through the door addressed to me with the National Health Service stamp showing on the outside. I opened it to find an appointment for a CAT scan the following week. This was a good service, I thought initially and wrote the appointment in my diary realising I would have to miss or move two meetings which would involve 10 other people, in order to keep the appointment. Hmmm, perhaps not so good with its assumptions about who is available for what and when. It was later that day that I began to think that maybe the appointment had come rather more quickly than I would have expected and then, being the anxious man that I am, I began to think that perhaps the neurologist did expect to find something and that the scan needed getting on with because it would need sorting. The words one dare not speak. Brain tumour! Yes, brain tumour had featured in my research as one of the causes of the symptom of tremor and I had chosen completely to ignore that possibility until now. All I could do at this juncture was to worry pointlessly and needlessly about the fact that I have had an excellent response from the National Health Service. Of course, I was worried that I might have a growth in my brain and had sat on that concern until it had been completely opened up by this letter. Now, it was the foremost thought in my mind and really did preoccupy me.

The day for the scan arrived. I drove from my office in Stretford to the Manchester Royal Infirmary where the scan was to take place. The staff were, as so many NHS staff are, extremely pleasant and professional. I was whisked into the waiting room, given a form to fill in, and asked to return it to the desk as soon as it was completed. It was simple to do and I returned it and saw it taken away by a nurse within moments. It must have been not more than five minutes before I was called through. I walked into a large room which was filled with a large, stumpy, fat tube lying on its side surrounded by monitors and sundry other pieces of equipment which I could not identify. There was a bed, well more of a board really, sticking out of the hole in the scanner and I was invited to lie on it. Someone explained to me that if I were claustrophobic I might find the scanner a little tight. I was then asked to lie still for about 10 minutes while the scan took place. I started to chuckle at this, then to laugh out loud and noted the consternation on the radiographers face.

"Well" I said, "I've been sent here because I shake so I can't guarantee to lie still for you although I will do my best"

"Oh sorry" he said. "Here, we can certainly help with that", and so saying he hurried off for a moment and returned with some foam wedges which he proceeded to tuck in particularly around my head. This was comfy.

They told me they were about to start the machine, so I shut my eyes and relaxed. They pulled a face guard down over my head. I could see what he meant about claustrophobic, as the table slid back slowly into the tube in the centre of the scanner. "Eyes wide shut" I thought. Imagine a beach, the sun is shining, music playing, the sea lapping against your feet. The claustrophobia faded away. I lay there quite happily for the 10 minutes it took for the various parts of the machine to bang and clatter through their complicated electronic processes. Then things went relatively quiet and the bed glided out of the machine. Friendly hands helped me to sit up and step down from the platform and I was invited to leave and await results "in due course".

Four weeks went by with no contact at all from the hospital. Although I had been worried, the reality of my life was that I was a very busy man and often would only worry when I was reminded to, such as when the tremor in my left arm kicked in. By now, this had changed from a tic to an undeniable tremor. That being said, it wasn't exactly having much effect on my life. So four weeks had passed quickly, as they usually did. My days were filled with running a busy probation and bail hostel as a senior probation officer. This was not a post in my service that I would ever have applied for but the hostel (the biggest in the North West) had not had a permanent manager for over two years and the chief officer sent me there because the absence of management impact had begun to show in a number of ways. It turned out to be a most enjoyable role, working with a very good team of colleagues. I even got involved in sorting out disputes with the neighbours, with whom I had considerable empathy. They were living next to what was, in some respects, like an open prison. Evenings and weekends were at home with my wife and two young, but energetic and rapidly growing teenage boys. In addition to this, my role included overnight or weekend on call functions, being available to the staff in all six of the hostels in Greater Manchester at those times who might need decisions about any number of different things which they would quite rightly see as being matters above their paygrade. However at the end of four weeks I decided that I really should've heard a result from the scan one way or another and so wrote to the consultant asking for an outcome and reminding him that he had said he would also organise an MRI scan.

Within a week I received a letter which nearly apologised for the gap in contact and did clarify that the CAT scan had been normal, although there was a small spot at the lower back of the brain which could indicate that I may have had a small stroke at some point. This was a shocking revelation in itself but the consultant said it was nothing to worry about and probably not relevant to the matter at hand. The letter went on to say that he had said he would consider an MRI scan and that he had now done so and was organising one for me. This was in the October. The appointment letter finally arrived in mid-January for March, the absence of a tumour having clearly put the brakes on the whole process, or at least that was how it felt. At one level, this felt quite reasonable. At another it still begged the question: 'of what was my tremor symptomatic?'

In 1994 March arrived quietly, as it does every year, slotting ever so neatly between February and April. The day for the scan loomed. I felt more or less like an old hand at scans, having had one, although I wasn't sure what the difference was between the CAT and the MRI except that the M in MRI stood for magnetic and it meant that there could be no metal within the vicinity of the equipment. I dressed carefully, as if for a first date, checking that fastenings and zippers were of plastic rather than metal so that I wouldn't have to take too many clothes off.

I drove from home to the North Manchester General Hospital as it was a morning appointment. This is not a place that I knew at all and I allowed myself plenty of time to find a parking space and make my way to the scanning facility. When I finally arrived there, I was impressed with the plushness of the unit which had clearly been specially built, and recently at that. It was now approximately a year since I first went to my GP and the time had passed very quickly. I couldn't tell if my tremor was worse but I thought it might be. I was still looking at Parkinson's rather than anything else as the likely diagnosis, but nevertheless, wanted to be told properly by the right person with the right knowledge.

Once again there were forms to fill in but this time they were indemnities in case I had any metal in my eye or other parts my body from a previous incident which might be ripped out by the magnetic field in the machine I was going to lie in. I thought carefully this time about the form and once again the answers were all negative. A member of staff then talked me through the procedure which was essentially the same as it had been for the CAT scan. I was escorted into the scanning room which was once again full of pieces of high-tech equipment. Most impressive of all however, was the actual scanner itself. It was almost skeletal in comparison to the machine at Manchester Royal infirmary. Instead of the bed sliding into an enclosed tube, the scanning part was like a doughnut around the platform, so making the whole process look as if it would be less claustrophobic.

I lay on the bed, explained again about my tremor and was again tucked in with sponge wedges. Although the face mask was much nearer to my face, my previous experience and the relative openness of this machine did make it less worrying. The other noticeable difference was how quiet this MRI scanner was in comparison to the CAT. One could be tempted to have a nap during this process.

Chapter 5 - Confirmation

It was 11 am on a bright and sunny Tuesday morning in July 1995. My mind was blank. I was waiting to be told what could be very bad news but I had no thoughts in my head of any use or relevance to the situation. Unusually for me, it was empty. A defence? Probably.

I was sitting in the waiting area at the outpatients department at the National Neurological Hospital in London waiting to see Dr Niall Quinn, a consultant neurologist who specialised in Parkinson's disease. I had been there about an hour and I was beginning to feel rather irritated at the wait, having not had any explanation offered as to its cause. I had got up at 5:30 so that I could leave home at 6:10 and get to Stockport station, parked up and onto the 07:03 to London Euston. It was then a relatively short walk up to Queens Square and into the hospital but I wanted to make sure I had plenty of time in case of getting lost, a practice in which I excel. As it turned out, I went straight to the correct place and was actually 22 minutes early for my 10 o'clock appointment. Finally word came that Mr Quinn had been due back from his holidays yesterday, that there had been a problem with transport and he had landed this morning. Knowing at least that he was due to arrive made the wait a little less irritating.

Finally at about 12:30 he swept into the Department and his first patient was called. I settled down to wait for yet another indeterminate period of time. In fact it was only about half hour before I was called and after the usual banter about the spelling and pronunciation of my surname, I was shown into his consulting room. He was a much younger man than I had expected and built like a rugby player. He had a more personable manner than the neurologist at Tameside. He referenced the letter that had been sent and asked me a few questions similar to those asked by everybody who I had seen about my tremor. He then put me through a series of physical exercises such as walking along the corridor outside the office and sitting and flapping my hands. For anybody who enjoys being paraded along the corridor in front of waiting patients or flapping their hands at a professional who is assessing you for a significant illness this would have been a joyful and not even slightly embarrassing interlude. I however, can't honestly say that I do enjoy such things. Nevertheless I did as instructed to find out whether I had passed the test! He invited me to sit and he took his place on the other side of the desk and made a shortlist of bullet points.

He looked at me and said "well, it is Parkinson's, but you knew that didn't you?" I looked at him and nodded vaguely. He went on to point out to me that I was required to notify the DVLA who would make a decision as to my ability to continue to hold a driving licence. He suggested I consider joining the Parkinson's Society and then said that he had agreed with my home neurologist's proposal for medication. He said that he would write back to Tameside Hospital and to my GP and they would organise the prescribing of medication for me.
"Will it shorten my life?" I blurted out over his desk.
He paused for longer than I had expected. "A little" he said quietly.
With that, the consultation was over.

I walked out of the hospital unable to get my brain in gear as far as making sense of what just happened. I carried on into

Queen's Square and walked down a side road, past the St Giles hotel, where my memory pulled back an abiding recollection of a two night stay, the focus of which was the miniscule size of the rooms. This was an easier thought than the implications of Parkinson's disease. I continued on to Southampton Row. In my dazed state, I turned right instead of left. It was a beautiful day and I wasn't paying any particular attention. Thinking that I had set myself on the correct path for getting to the Home Office at Queen Anne's Gate, where I was based, I strolled instead along past Russell Square and on to Woburn Place.

It was here that I spotted the sign for the Parkinson's Disease Society head office. It was as if I had been pulled by a tractor beam. The sign registered through my dream state no doubt because of the comment made by Dr Quinn. I went through the door and found myself in a rather dingy, poky room. The young woman behind the counter looked at me and asked what she could do for me. I said that I would like to join and wondered if there was anyone I could talk to. Initially she looked rather flustered and it suddenly occurred to me that most new members joined by post and very few would actually turn up to buy their membership. Despite the slightly strange nature of the request, she asked me to wait and disappeared through a narrow doorway, returning a few minutes later and asking me to take a seat. Shortly after that, a very pleasant woman appeared, greeted me and asked how she could help. I explained what had just happened and said that I thought I ought to join as one day I might need some help. Little did I know then just how significant the work of the society would become. I was duly sorted out with membership and agreed to pay £10 per quarter via standing order. Having pulled myself together, I left the office through the door by which I had entered and correctly turned right. I headed off, with a little more determination than earlier, towards my workplace.

I stopped about halfway and sat in a cafe for a late lunch and a brew. I couldn't really think about what I had been told. It was too big and too complicated and despite everything, too unreal. So I ate with my usual gusto, polishing off an egg mayonnaise sandwich and two large mugs of tea. After that, I finished my walk to the Home Office in about 10 minutes and took the lift up to the seventh floor and went into our office.

Tony, my line manager was in the room but everybody else was out. Not being at all subtle about these things I told Tony about the diagnosis. He was shocked and sympathetic, but it was a short discussion simply because I had not been able to think through any implications or identify whether or not I actually needed to do anything. I phoned home to describe everything that had gone on. It was something of a relief to share that, although the same time I felt guilty about putting the burden on Dot. Neither of us is given to dramatics, hysterics or overreactions. I think we're both quite philosophical and are less inclined to ask 'why me' and are more likely to wonder quietly 'why not me'. I then thought I ought to do some work but found myself unable to decide what I should do and quite frankly uninterested in doing anything.

My 'health journey' to this point, the confirmation of diagnosis had taken something over two years, not an uncommon time and by no means an unusually long one to get a confirmed diagnosis. There is a theory amongst the Parkinson's community (there are many theories amongst the Parkinson's community), but there is one in particular about what causes the condition to establish itself. This is what I term the Bodyshock Theory. The basis is that something happens of significance, which, as a secondary consequence, causes the dopamine producing cells in the brain to die off. Now, I'm not saying that I think this idea is right or wrong. Most people I have asked can think of something. But it is very difficult to assess the scale of one person's event against another. In my case it was very easy to track back to a possible body shock event which I think most people would acknowledge as being of significance.

In 1989 our third son, Conrad, had died during his birth. That experience could be a whole book in itself. Suffice to say that if I had to identify something that had knocked me sideways in a way that I can scarcely describe or bear to think about, that was it and this is how it happened:

She looked at me across the living room "it's time". "Is it?" I asked though I don't know why. She would know if her waters broke, but it's just the way these conversations go. Our third child, much heralded, deeply anticipated and much loved even though we didn't know yet whether it would be a he or she. We moved into action like the well-oiled machine we were. What would now be called a birthing plan, but which we just called the list, needed to be enacted. First thing was to get the boys over to the Jones's. They were well aware of their parts of the plan. When I called them from play and told them that the baby had started to come and I needed to take Dot to the hospital, they knew that they were going to stay overnight at their friends house. They had little bags ready with what they would need and they were as excited as we were, tinged also, as for us, in their own little ways, with anticipation. I got them in the car after they had had a hug and a kiss from Dot.

We made the short drive in 10 minutes and I bundled them into Cynthia's house where the excitement spread. I had a brief chat with Cynthia. Unfortunately Alan wasn't yet home so I couldn't share any jokes with him. By the time I got home Dot had already phoned the delivery unit at Tameside hospital and alerted them to expect us in the not too distant future.

"Do You think we should go or would you rather stay home awhile?" I asked. "We could have a brew before we go if you like".

"No, let's go" she said. "I just remember how quick Richard was and I don't want it happening in the car again." "Good point" I said as I lifted her bag into the boot of the car. She told me that her contractions were firm and regular but not particularly frequent. However we know how that can change and so after checking that the house was locked I helped her into the back seat so that she had some room to move around if needed.

The drive to the local hospital could be done in 20 minutes if there was no traffic. It took more like 35 minutes at that part of the day given the beginning of rush-hour and some roadworks en route. By the time I reached the maternity unit door, contractions had built up a little but were still some time from full-strength high-frequency. I got Dot inside and seated at the registration desk and I went back to move the car onto

38

the nearest car park. By the time I came back she had been taken off into a room where various forms were being filled in and records gathered. I went to join her and settled in for what I knew could be a lengthy wait.

It wasn't long before the contractions were coming hard and fast. Something had changed, but I had missed whatever it was that caused it. The atmosphere became still or perhaps tense is the better descriptor. Staff started to look a little concerned or worried and there were now several midwives in our room. Dot asked for more pain relief, and the answer was as far as I could make out 'let's just get baby out dear'. I know I was getting anxious, not getting answers to my questions. Three or four more people had come into the room whilst this last few minutes had gone by. I asked who they were and at that point one was introduced to us as a colleague from the SCUBA unit. We both knew that was the special care baby unit so we knew something was wrong but we had no idea what. Whilst this was going on the baby's head was crowning and the midwives were trying desperately to get the cord from round his neck. I couldn't tear my eyes away. I knew what it meant, or so I thought, possible oxygen starvation. This could get difficult. No sooner was he (so we now knew it was Conrad) out from Dot's body than the nurses had taken him away across the room and I could see that they were giving cardiac resuscitation. More staff arrived I couldn't see too much. I was holding Dot's hand. We were both watching and waiting to be given our child back. At that point I saw what looked like an enormous syringe being plunged into his chest and I knew that we were in serious territory. I still had no idea just how serious. Dot of course was exhausted with the efforts of giving birth to what had certainly been a life just a few minutes ago. One of the team brought our inappropriately silent little man over to us and said "I'm so sorry"... I can only remember yelling. I have no idea what I said. Dot was busy examining Conrad and of course we were both in tears. She held him for quite a while and then the midwife said "let me take him for a few minutes. I'll clean him up and bring him back to you."

It didn't take long to bring him back clean and dressed and looking every inch like our third child ought to look. I can't describe the state that my head was in and I guess Dot was in a similar limbo. I honestly expected him to wake up. After a while staff numbers had reduced to a reasonable group who brought us a camera and suggested we might like to take pictures, which of course we did and probably wouldn't have thought of doing had they not been suggested.

I held him in my arms and walked around the delivery suite gently rocking him and talking to him, urging him to waken from the dark, dark place that he dropped into. But it wasn't to be. I felt him go cold and at that point decided that it was very, very real. I hugged Dot and then doctors came to speak to me and asked me to step outside of the room.

I asked them what had happened and they were honest enough to say they didn't know. They thought that his heart might have been in the wrong place as he hadn't responded to the injections of adrenaline which they had been trying to put straight into the heart. They then asked me for permission to conduct an autopsy. I felt sick but said yes because I needed to know what happened. One minute alive and kicking literally. Next minute, going cold. It's hard to credit. He also looked exactly like Matthew had done. There was no doubting that this was my third son and we deserved to know what had happened to him.

After some hours, at about 2 am I decided I needed to sleep. I said to Dot that I was going to go home for a while to sort things out and start to let people know. The midwives wanted her to stay in overnight although she did not want to. I had no fight left and I thought it might be best for her anyway to be there and resting as I knew that once she got home she wouldn't and her body had been battered as well as her mind. I didn't know how we'd manage this. It felt bigger than anything I'd faced before and I had no plan at all. I have to admit that despite my various life experiences I hadn't considered this option for a minute. I did know that we would get through it though and I was also confident we would emerge on the other side functional, if rather damaged.

I drove home through the dark quiet streets barely able to believe what had happened. I was at a loss as to what I should do in what order and on whom I could rely to help me to deal with this unexpected and very unwelcome tragedy. I pulled up outside the house. On automatic pilot I went in and started making a cup of tea. I sat down on the sofa and woke up an hour later. I crawled upstairs and as I walked into our bedroom was beaten in the face by the sight of the Moses crib sitting at the end of our bed waiting for our beautiful third child, now never to be able to fulfil that last role for us. I dropped onto the bed and started to cry. I woke up at 6:30 and got up. I had things to do I just wasn't sure what they were. So I decided to call in on my friendship with Wasyl again as I had done more than once before. He was shocked and upset and promised to get over as soon as possible and I knew he would do that.

I made short phone calls to a few family members. I told them the briefest of facts and that I would be back in touch later on in the day. Now, I had to face one of the worst parts of the whole business. My two little boys aged seven and six were waiting for me at their friend's home wanting to hear all about their new brother or sister. And I had to go and tell them what had happened. I drove across town feeling sick and with a weight in my stomach. The detail of what happened that morning is covered later on as I can make more sense of it in that part of the story. Suffice to say that it was a surreal experience for me and I have no idea if I handled it well or not. The main point is that I handled it and between us all and over time, we managed to regain some equilibrium.

Jumping back to the day of my diagnosis, it was a hot, bright, blue sky-ed, sunny day in July 1995. I was 39 and would be 40 in a few weeks. It was almost five years since I had carried Conrad's tiny pine coffin across the rough ground of Moston Cemetery in north Manchester. Maybe that was a "Body Shock" start point. Maybe it wasn't. I don't know and perhaps will never find out. The night of his burial, when family and friends had left us and we had got the boys to bed, I looked out at the pouring rain and felt the broken pieces of my heart get ground into powder. I sobbed long and loud. I felt wretched and climbed fully clothed into the bath, and curled up into a ball, stifling my sobs for fear of wakening the two boys and turning the shower cold on my head. Yes, that had certainly been a body shock and a brain shock and yes, except for this part of that awful day I took on my usual role of sorter outer, carer, getter done of things, attender to everybody's needs and provider of solace and comfort. That was my way of avoiding being needy.

Back in my office after diagnosis, my brain full of Parkinson's thoughts, I realised that I was unable to focus on my work and realistically shouldn't be there. I took a slightly earlier train home that night, amazed at how weary I felt, picked up the car from the car park at Stockport station and drove home rather on autopilot. The boys were in bed and Dot was in the kitchen. I walked in and experienced that wonderful coming home feeling. Dot walked over and put her arms round me at which point I cried for about 30 seconds. I decided then that I wasn't going to be miserable but was going to fight all the way, whatever that meant. Little did I know then just how difficult it would be not to weep, in part because of the things that would happen to me and also because Parkinson's can so easily make a person highly emotional.

Chapter 6 – Spreading the Word

I woke up the morning after my now confirmed diagnosis and lay in bed thinking. Nothing felt any different and yet my life in theory had been turned upside down. Well, carpe diem. I got up and set about my daily routine. Routine is a bit of a strong word to describe my days. Although for many years I did have a job which involved commuting to the same office each day, it certainly never required me to be there at a specific time other than that at which a particular activity might be occurring. As a probation officer that might involve being at court for a certain time or having an appointment at a prison to conduct an interview. As a senior probation officer, my grade at that time, it might be a meeting at the office or elsewhere. Once again, starting times would vary and so the time I would have to leave home varied accordingly.

At the time I am writing about – diagnosis time (1995) - I was on secondment to the Home Office to help with the implementation of a national information system for the probation service in England and Wales. It was a home-based job effectively and so there was no commuting other than the two steps from my bed to my desk. Equally however I might be required to be in South Wales or any other part of England and Wales for a 10 o'clock start. Sometimes I'd be away overnight. Sometimes I'd leave very early and return very late. This suited me quite well and above all it was different. It involved me working with senior managers. I was learning for my next career move. I was actively involved in Home Office circles so picked up about civil service and political issues. As the project was about IT and information systems, I was developing an understanding of information needs and flows and possibilities as well as learning more about how to use a computer. A good job from my point of view.

My immediate colleagues were a friendly bunch. We got on well and worked well together. I had no qualms about telling them about my condition and knew that I would do that whenever I would next see them. That could be anywhere between one and four weeks. Before that however, I needed to let my family know. I rang my sister, Sheila, first. She is 18 months younger than me. As kids at home we had a typical love hate relationship that went through the ups and downs of rowing, of fighting and of tolerating each other. As adults we get on well and I would describe us as a very close family. I decided to speak to her first as I thought she would be the easiest one to tell, in that I knew she would be concerned for me and sympathetic but wouldn't be pushy or ask difficult questions. We chatted for a while and I came out with it. She cried and I didn't know what to do with myself. I felt awful for having upset her even though I know that's a ridiculous response. We talked a little longer and I made my excuses and came off the phone, knowing that the conversation would be picked up in the not too distant future.

I decided to wait until the evening to speak to my brother. Paul is three years older than me, and apart from our physical appearance we are different in so very many ways. He is a very sociable, gregarious man who is at the centre of any social gathering. He carries the role of "Big Brother" lightly, but you know if push comes to shove that he'll be there and do what needs doing. There were man issues to be considered such as not talking too much about feelings and not showing anxiety, fear or other "stereotypical weakness". I can, of course, do these things but generally prefer not to. Although we are close as brothers, we don't have lots in common in terms of taste or activities. I rang him, not a frequent occurrence, and could hear the enquiry in his voice on hearing that it was me on the phone. Again we chatted a little. He knew that I had been to the doctor's with the tremor and so I moved on quickly to saying that I had been to see the specialist. The conversation took a fairly serious turn as I explained as best I could what it meant. Once I had cleared the hurdle of clarifying that it wasn't fatal the mood lightened and he made a joke about finding some use for the tremor! It was good and comforting to know that I wouldn't be the only one laughing at whatever it was that was going to happen. I had asked both my brother and sister not to mention it to our mother as I needed to do that myself. I wasn't sure of the best way of doing it however and so didn't immediately do anything.

It was a couple more weeks before I had settled on a strategy. I didn't want mum to be upset as much for me as for her. At the same time I didn't want to limit talk about it and I knew I would need to answer any questions if I could. No point in doing it in her house where she lived with her elder sister, Aunty Eileen who, delightful as she was, didn't feature in this scenario. So, I phoned one evening to chat and ended up inviting mum to join me for lunch the following day. She sounded really pleased, which was a good start and we agreed a time and left it there. I invited her to pick the venue which again, she seemed happy to do. I hadn't worked out my words so my brain was going over time as I drove to pick her up. We set off straight away and drove into central Manchester. I parked at the Blackfriars car park and we walked across

Deansgate and through St Ann's Square to the shopping arcade. Downstairs, there used to be a few restaurants and mum was particularly keen on one of them. That suited me fine.

We had a table with a reasonable amount of space around it and no pressure from crowds to give up one's table the moment one had finished eating. We ordered the food which duly arrived complete with pots of tea and we chatted easily enough about the family, work, various friends and so forth. I wasn't sure whether I should say something now, nor how to lead into it and so rather abruptly after we finished eating but whilst still drinking tea I said "I have some news. I may not be as well as you would like." I realised as soon as I spoke that this was a far more alarming start than required and far more than I wanted to achieve.

"What do you mean?" she queried.

"It seems that I have Parkinson's Disease". The silence was fairly long and I could see her wrestling with emotions and questions. I had been right about the neutral venue in public. She held herself together well. She asked me what had been going on and I gave a brief outline of the trips to the consultants, the scans, what they had told me about what they were going to do about it. I then briefly explained that I wasn't completely clear but that drugs would feature for the rest of my life. I made the point that it was degenerative. Mum told me about a friend of hers from Clones, the Irish border town of her birth, who suffered from the same condition. I quickly pointed out that it was different for everybody just in case her friend has had a particularly bad time. I could see she was upset but talked quietly with her, answering a few more questions that she had, including whether or not I had told my brother and sister. I think it helped that I had saved her from having to do it. She asked me how I was feeling. I felt pretty rotten for having to tell her and not having the bottle to tell her at home, which probably would have been perfectly fine. On the other hand we had enjoyed going out for lunch together and me paying the bill.

Chapter 7 – Parents

Mum is in fact a remarkable woman in many ways. She grew up one of 10 children. The family lived in Clones – her home town in Co Monaghan Eire, a small border town in the Irish Republic. She came to England in 1945, when she was 20, to help to look after her eldest sister's toddler whilst the second child was born. She came here for a few weeks only and has been here now over 70 years.

My aunt –Anna Frances, but universally known as Nancy - lived in Buxton, Derbyshire and it was here that mum met my father. He too was an immigrant, but had travelled a very different route to get to the same place. Born and raised one of nine children from a small Polish village called Miejsce Piastowe, in the south-eastern region of Poland, an area known as the sub-Carpathian mountains. He was unfortunate enough to be in the middle of his National Service when war was declared. He was marched out of Poland to fight with the allies, although he was in fact caught and held as a prisoner of war for most of the time. Whilst this wasn't anything like being in the concentration camps, he was worked very hard in farm work and fed very little. Once peace had been declared he was discharged but like all other Polish personnel was not able to return to the land of his birth because of the Russian stance. Thus he was demobbed and after a holiday in Italy travelled to England and was located at a camp in Buxton. Although he had been training as a bookbinder prior to his National Service, he was given work in the quarries around Buxton and he was known as a hard worker as far as I can establish.

Mum's given names are Josephine Patricia. She is however, known universally and affectionately as Paddy. The name came from her christening day. Her godfather, old Seamus Cullinan, (the father of young Seamus Cullinan who came to lodge with us for several years, whilst working for the GPO in Manchester, until he married Eileen Quinn the daughter of one of our neighbours) liked to have a flutter on the horses. On the day of mum's christening there was a horse running named Paddy and Seamus said to my grandfather that, should the horse win, given that he had placed a five pound bet on it, my mum would henceforth be called Paddy. And so it came to be.

The parish church of St Anne's in Buxton was where mum went to worship. Here, the parish priest would regularly comment during his sermons about the importance of the local population paying attention to those Poles and others who had been unable to return home. He encouraged local people to fraternise with them and to attend the camp's Saturday night dances and to make the visitors feel welcome.

Mum and her friends, all single, all in their early 20s, needed little encouragement. The Saturday night dance was a highlight of the week. My dad at that time spoke little or no English and danced, I am told, rather like an elephant with blisters. That being said, he took an early fancy to my mother and when she arrived on a Saturday evening he would approach asking her to dance. It got to the point where she felt very conflicted. On the one hand she enjoyed his company and found him attractive. On the other, she liked to dance but that was not what she called what he did.

Anyway, love conquers all as they say, and despite these early difficulties they became close and eventually a couple. He proposed to her and she accepted. They were married in St Anne's Church in Buxton on the 21st July 1951. Two strangers in a foreign land, embarking on an exciting life journey, with no idea of the joys and tribulation to come.

Dad worked hard, as many of the immigrant Poles did, to support his family. Having moved to Manchester, he got work as a scaffolder during the day and resisted the laughter and derision of work colleagues and their pressure to join them in the pub drinking every night. Instead, he pointed out to them that he was saving up to put a deposit on a house. He worked several evenings a week as a waiter and barman in The Brunswick pub named after the area it was in and the street it was on. He moved from there to work in the Lloyds Pub in Chorlton, which is still there and doing good business. There were a number of Polish men, couples and indeed families living around the district known as Victoria Park, sandwiched between Longsight and Rusholme. My dad had become very friendly with a couple of others and between them they bought houses one after the other, each one accommodating friends as best they could until they bought their own place and moved on. This is, in many ways, the story of immigrants the world over. In November 1952, my brother was born and not long after that dad managed to buy his first house with a mortgage. He also took out life insurance much to my mother's concern, as that meant less cash to fill the shopping basket each week. However my dad was adamant that it was the right thing to do and just got on with it. I came along in August 1955 and my sister in February 1957. We were now well settled as a family in Victoria Park. We lived in a modestly sized Victorian terraced house on a street where it was safe for the children to play out. Dad was still working two jobs to maintain the family in a reasonable lifestyle, at which he was very successful. A number of my mother's siblings had come across from Ireland and settled in and around Manchester. Some of them lived with us for a time although I don't have any actual memory of that. There was no loss of contact with the extended family which was all of the Irish side, as well as lots of social contact with other Polish families who lived in the area. I always felt it a pity that we were not taught to speak Polish at our father's knee.

Since being aged 19, in 1938 when he was conscripted, dad's only contact with his own family had been by letter. He was now in a position to try and do something about it and arranged for his mother to come to England in the summer of 1958. This would reunite him with her and allow her to meet her daughter-in-law and three grandchildren about whom she had heard plenty, but, of course, had never met. This was at a time when travelling from south-east Poland to Manchester would take 2 to 3 days of complicated arrangements which would be wearing and problematic, the more so if the traveller was unable to speak English. And so it was, early in 1958 that Babcia (Grandma) Wegrzyn, despite the desire to see her son and his family, realised that her frailty and the complexity of the journey meant that she could not manage the trip, even if her youngest daughter accompanied her. This was a huge disappointment to my dad. He understood his mum's position of course. Accordingly, he wrote to her and said that he would take British citizenship (something he had never wanted to do, as he was unsure if it would make for added difficulties should he be able to leave England for

Poland in the future and want to return). He suggested that in the summer of the following year 1959, he would travel to Poland with my brother and I. I'm not at all sure he'd thought that one through, as we would have been seven and four respectively and he would have been a man on his own travelling on buses, train and boat for two or three days. Anyway his sentiment was clear; he wanted to see his mum and for his mum to meet her grandchildren to the extent that that was possible to arrange.

On 7th November 1958 having spent the day scaffolding, dad came home and drank his usual pint of sour milk, had his tea, got washed and changed and after a few minutes playing with us in our beds set off on his bike to work in the pub. He never returned. At a few minutes past midnight that night, while cycling along Hathersage Road on his way home, he was hit by a van. His head hit the floor and he suffered severe skull fractures and brain damage. He survived for four hours on a ward at Manchester Royal Infirmary and then died without regaining consciousness.

It wasn't until nearly 6 o'clock in the morning that the police arrived to break the news to mum. She had been sick with worry since about half past one that morning but with no telephone and three children aged 6, 3 and 1 1/2 asleep in bed there was little she could do. The police were fairly abrasive with her, partly I'm sure because she is Irish and partly because she had not phoned them and it had been difficult to track her down as dad had not had any ID papers on him. In fact, it was thanks to a photograph in his wallet of the staff at the Brunswick pub where dad used to work that police were able to trace the family. Officers had recognised the landlord of the pub in the photograph and went round. The reason dad had been late leaving the Lloyd's pub in Chorlton, to which he had moved some time before and where he was working along with uncle Owen and a couple of friends from the neighbourhood, was because his former boss had called in for a drink at the end of the night. He was a great friend of dad's and one of the few people that would cause him to stay behind after work for a drink. It was his wife however who looked at the photograph when the police called and pointed dad out and went into the hospital to identify him.

So, as a result of a moment's carelessness by the driver, a good man's life is lost at the age of 39; three children face growing up without a father; a mother never gets to see her son again after 20 years; and a woman, wife and mother loses her man, her partner and her support and is left to manage as best she can. And my future was changed. Of that I have no doubt. I just don't know in what way it was changed.

On top of the singular tragedy of such an occurrence, the things that are lost which are not obvious include knowing whether or not a person carried any genetic disposition. I have no idea whether my dad might have developed Parkinson's disease, young or old onset. Had I known, it probably would not have made any difference. Without a doubt his loss and absence from my life has had a major effect on forming me and on some of the decisions that I made and the attitudes that I hold as a result, have remained important throughout my life.

Notwithstanding any of that, had he lived would not have made any difference, I believe, in terms of whether or not I developed Parkinson's disease. What it may have made a difference to is my philosophy of life. One of my biggest regrets in life is not knowing my father and never having had a chance to talk to him about his experiences. I get what I can from people who knew him but it's thin in comparison to an actual contact and it lacks the detail that only those involved can provide, talking about emotions as well as events.

Growing up without a father and knowing that he went out one morning and simply didn't return does give you a strong sense of not expecting everything to work out well. I can remember in my teenage years thinking this through. I won't pretend it was easy, but I realised that expecting everything would work out as planned was probably doomed to failure, as I knew from my own experience that this was not what happened. On the other hand if things did work out then they had gone beyond expectation and that was always a delight. By the same measure it can make it hard sometimes to make the big decisions because at the back of one's mind is the thought that this won't work out and so what's the point in getting into it?

I guess this is the philosophy that is behind my not asking 'why me' when I was diagnosed, because 'why not me' reflects my perspective. I guess I might overthink this sometimes but on reflection I do find that I don't have a 'why me' attitude about anything. I realise that this may sound maudlin or unduly negative, but it really isn't so.

The other attitudinal aspect that I think relates back to this, and perhaps other times in my life is to dismiss things with "it could be worse". This undoubtedly helps me to take a more balanced perspective than I might otherwise on a number of aspects of life, health being one of them. I have never found it difficult to imagine far worse health problems than I have experienced being dealt with by somebody at any particular time, whether it's anybody I know or not. It also applies across types of issue. The loss of Conrad was a terrible experience but it's not too hard to imagine worse things going on in life and to feel guilty relief that one only has to deal with whatever it is that's in front of you.

Chapter 8 - Education

I had excellent educational opportunity as a child but did not make the most of it by a long chalk. I'm sure it was not helped by the absence of my father. We all went to the local primary school and all did reasonably well there. One of my earliest school memories is of being summonsed from the reception class one day and taken into the next class, Infants 1, and told to sit and that this would henceforth be my classroom. I was put on the middle table and had no understanding at all as to why I had been taken from my friends. Fortunately, there were one or two children in the class that I knew and played with outside of school and that helped soften the discomfort. Of course it was simply because of where birthdays fell. Mine, being 30 August meant that I was in the correct class for my age, albeit I would be almost automatically the youngest in the class by far and there would be children almost a year older in the same class. Of course this meant nothing to me I just got my head down and got on. The teacher, Mrs Harvey, was pleasant and I knew her already, as she and her family lived on our road. This made things a little easier as well. So I got over the slight upset at being moved and got stuck into some actual work in this class rather than play all day. I could already read and write to some extent and can remember going through Primary School relatively easily and always at the top of my class. It certainly didn't take me long in Mrs Harvey's class to get off the middle table onto the top table.

By the time it got to 1965, (Junior four or Year 6 in modern education), the school year in which I would become 11 and therefore the last year of primary school, it was simply recognised that I was performing at a high level. I can remember on one occasion the class being moved into groups by the teacher, Mr Willoughby who was known as "Pop". He was a remarkably good man and did a tremendous amount for me and my family, leaving us anonymous Christmas boxes every year and taking me out to concerts and other such events to help my development and in recognition of the absence of a father figure I think. He was a bachelor who lived with his spinster sister, also a teacher. There was nothing remotely untoward about the attention and consideration he lavished on me, he was simply a good man.

Having divided the class into groups, the purpose of the division became clear and I suddenly understood why I was sitting at a table with eight children who I would normally have little to do with. One child in each group was designated as leader. The groups were reading groups and it was the leader's role to listen to each member in turn and correct their reading. Of course, this sort of division is not a good approach in many ways, but at the time, the very early sixties, even before the Beatles really hit the big time, the general approach to education was competitive and most children got stuck in. It was harder for those who struggled to achieve, but for me, it was a fairly straightforward groove to follow. I can recall feeling uncomfortable with the task. Even more, I can recall feeling shocked when I listened to the first of my peers, a lad called David Farrell who was a perfectly pleasant, quiet boy struggling to read a very simple English sentence. I truly believe that that moment was one of my formative experiences and without being at the front of my mind very much at all, was one of the drivers that took me into public service.

This was also the year of the 11+ plus examination, which we all took, even those who like me were only 10 and a half. I have no intention at all of examining the merits and demerits of this particular form of discrimination. That's a whole other issue. It was what we did at that age and we all did it and were expected to do as well as possible. I have no recollection of cramming for the exam but I did work for it and it was fairly clear to me that the expectation was that I would pass for grammar schools. That was fine by me, I knew no better. The first exam day came around and we all walked, crocodile style, from our school the relatively short distance to Pope Pius, a secondary modern school where the exam was to be held and where many primary school children were walking to on that day. The 11+ was a formal examination properly regulated and with strict rules about start and finish. I listened to the invigilator, followed the instructions, and at the appointed moment I began. The questions were like the questions we had been doing for homework and most I thought were fairly easy, with a few requiring some thinking or a bit of effort. I do remember finishing the exams within the time allowed although not necessarily by any large amounts of time. A few weeks later the results were published and I discovered that I had passed for grammar school and would be able to go to Xaverian College. The great thing about this from my point of view was that the school was only five minutes away from home with a range of short walks covering different routes or even shorter bicycle rides to and from school and not having to get on a bus crowded with others.

Before finishing primary school and starting at Xaverian, I had a strange experience which has also had a lifelong impact. One day a priest came into Mr Willoughby's classroom. He was introduced to us as a White Father. This was not a reference to his skin colour. It was the name of the order to which he belonged. He had come to tell us about his work as a missionary priest in Africa and we listened with various levels of interest to the tales he told for a short period of time. He then asked a few questions and made a number of comments, partly interacting directly with the children and also at times with Pop Willoughby. After a little while he asked Pop whether there were any potential priests in the class and to my complete amazement I was named. What an odd moment. On one hand flattered to be identified as a potential priest and all that went with that role (as I understood it at that age) within the Catholic Church. On the other, I was shocked to be identified as a potential priest. One who would live a life of spirituality, poverty and might end up working as a missionary in Africa. The White Father, never one to miss an opportunity for recruiting asked me if I would like to visit the seminary in Grange over Sands near the Lake District. I was not brought up to say 'no' to priests, so I said 'yes'.

This "arrangement" was followed up at home very quickly. Mum received a visit from the priest and the parish priest who put in place the arrangements needed to go up to the seminary immediately the summer holidays began. After this was all agreed to, mum talked to me about it and asked me if I wanted to go. I said I didn't mind. At the time I didn't know whether I did or didn't mind but it was interesting to have that much attention being paid. Mum was very pleased I think.

I don't remember an awful lot of detail about my time in the seminary. I remember being there and the weather being lovely and sunny and the food being different but plentiful.

The staff were very pleasant and the other boys were a mixed bunch from the sublime to the ridiculous as you would expect. There were a lot of prayers and we slept in dormitories which I didn't like. I can remember crying myself to sleep on one occasion, though I have no memory of why and when one of the staff came to check on me I just said everything was fine. After three or four weeks, we were all called for individual interviews with the boss of the seminary. As best I can remember the questions were fairly general. 'How have you got on? How was the food? Did you make any friends? Would you like to stay here?' And this is where I fell over. I had had enough during the time I was there to realise that I didn't want to stay there and be separated from family and I said so. It caused no problem. Arrangements were made for me to go home as planned at the end of the temporary stay and nothing would be followed up as I didn't want to return. I went home as arranged and told mum who I think was a little relieved as well as maybe a tad disappointed. Later in life I realised that life in the priesthood, the life of a celibate, was not for me at all. I would have been okay at the counselling and the gathering the youth together. I would have learned to manage dealing with death and the dying. I would have been good at confession and forgiveness. But I wouldn't have been any good at celibacy.

And so my life at junior school came to an end on something of a flat note I suppose. I had done well at primary school and learned later in life that mum had been told that I had passed my 11+ with the highest marks in the region. Great things that were expected of me. Interesting situation to be in when nobody tells you that. I think that if people want to have great expectations they should tell the person they expect from.

There would then be at least a fighting chance that people will be facing in the same direction. Grammar School was going to be a very different experience to that of primary education.

I digress. I had started to tell you about what a remarkable woman my mother is. Finding herself at 34, in a foreign country, widowed, with three children under eight years of age and with no income, it would not have been surprising if she had simply said "I can't cope" and left us to the welfare services.

Chapter 9 – My Mum

Although it might not have surprised some people, giving up in that way would have been completely against her ethics and her nature I suspect. There was no way on earth that this woman would lose her children as well as her husband, come what may. Instead, she showed a side of her character seldom seen. The tigress.

Her brother and sisters and others managed to persuade her that she should make a claim for financial support from the authorities, - no mean feat, given her reluctance to 'become dependant' by all accounts. After all, her siblings asked her rhetorically, how much would it cost them if you did put the children in care? So having finally succumbed to their sensible logic she filled in the relevant forms and sent them off. Some time afterwards she received a notification that she would receive the payment of 2/6d per week for the maintenance of the three of us. (that was half a crown – 12.5 pence in today's money). This was in 1959 and of course prices were considerably lower. However, even I can work out that notwithstanding widow's pension and child benefit, feeding, clothing and shelter for four humans would be a challenge for anybody and half a crown per week, was not going to make a significant difference compared to the income my father had generated. The tigress was unleashed. Mum marched down to the town hall and insisted on seeing the men responsible. There were two of them and she was on her own. But they didn't stand a chance. They had come between tigress and cubs and they were not going to get away with it. Mum used words and intonation not fists or aggression. How much did they think she could buy for two shillings and sixpence per week? How far would that go to alleviating the position? What would they do in those circumstances? Did they have any idea what she was going through? Never mind the grief and the loneliness and isolation of living where she did and the incessant demands of three growing little ones who could only identify what they wanted and express it noisily.

She then fell back on the argument used on her, took a deep breath and said "well, there's only one thing for it. I shall have to take a job and start earning money and saving it. In the meantime I shall have to put my three children into care and get them back when I saved up enough money to manage. You can work out how much that will cost you." And with that she left and returned home shaking all the way and desperately hoping that they did not call her bluff. She had no intention whatsoever of following through with it. Two days later a letter arrived from the town hall notifying her that her allowance was being increased to six shillings a week with immediate effect.

Until Sheila reached school age mum didn't consider taking a job. She budgeted brilliantly and kept us all fed and clothed and the house going. That she had a house to dwell in was of course testament to my dad's good sense in taking out insurance. Mum would not have and then would have had to find rent every week – no small task. She had some help from family and friends and I don't want to belittle that, it was much appreciated. But it was her drive and clear intent that we would grow up missing as little as possible of what she wanted as part of a normal life for us. I know she had many nights of tears for a long time after my dad was killed but they were never in front of us and we never wanted for her love and attention. The invaluable lesson here for me, and therefore to my approach to living with Parkinson's, is that you are responsible for your life, whatever is thrown at you. You are capable and responsible for accommodating it or otherwise dealing with it and ensuring that your life carries on in the way that you always intended, to the best of your ability.

Once Sheila had started school it was logical that mum got a job in the school as a classroom assistant. This meant that she could see us all off to school in the morning, be there when we got home in the evening, and have school holidays free. Again, an obvious path to take, which demanded that she talked to the right people and possess the right skills which she clearly had been able to demonstrate. After working for a few years, the opportunity to qualify as a nursery nurse came along. This was a two-year course which involved attendance at college and practice blocks in a variety of nursery settings. This meant that for the first time in our lives, she might not be there to see us out in the morning and when we got home from school. We were in our early teens and clearly this was something she was concerned about. The solution to this, reached in a way that I don't know, was to arrange for her older sister, aunty Clare to come and live with us.

Clare was a spinster who worked as the manager of a club in South Derbyshire. She was strongly opinionated, knew what was right, and would brook no nonsense from a trio of teenagers notwithstanding that she loved us to bits. It was an arrangement that was doomed to fail. We could not accept her absolute confidence that she was right and she could not accept our consequent failure to accept her authority. I honestly think she didn't realise that that was the issue nor that we were resentful of the way she went about things rather than what it was she went about. This was where her lack of experience with children showed itself most acutely I think. She expected us to act as if we were little adults and did not recognise the turbulence of the teens.

Nor did we, in all honesty, appreciate that this was an arrangement mum had entered into to ease her mind about our welfare while she bettered herself on the nursery nurse course. It was only years later that I discovered for example that Clare had given her money over the years to help her out. Generosity not often found even in close families.

So before the two years of the course was up, Claire's bags were packed and she left to go back to Melton Mowbray. We felt both jubilant and awkward. We knew that it was our behaviour and attitude towards her that had caused her to go but in all honesty it was liberating. Poor mum however had to figure out what she would do. She still had a block of time to go on her course and we were still young teenagers faced with the prospect of getting ourselves out and back into the house each day of the week. We pressed to be allowed to manage ourselves. And we won that particular debate.

Chapter 10 – Life's Philosophy

So how have these events shaped me? How have they helped me to form a philosophy of life? How do I know it is from these sources that my philosophy has evolved? I can't answer that. It may not be so. A forensic analysis, a surgical dissection if you like, of the cause and effect around my own, still rather mixed up approach to life, may or may not draw threads back to these events. It may draw them off in the opposite direction or move around them and factor in many other influences of which I remain blissfully unaware.

What is the philosophy that I think tracks back to these sources? On the whole I am an easy-going guy. That has not always been the case. Nowadays one of my favourite sayings is "well, it could be worse". This is without a doubt one of my mum's inconsistently applied approaches to life. However when it is applied, it is applied with rigour and across the board. It is well illustrated I think by this story.

A cold and damp November Saturday. I have decided to travel to Moston Cemetery in north Manchester to tidy up the grave that Conrad shares with his grandad. My decision is heavily influenced by the fact that November 8 is my dad's anniversary and it's always nice to have some acknowledgement of that event for mum. Accordingly, I phoned her and invited to come along with me and Matt and Richard. I guess the boys were about 11 or 12 so it was five or six years after Conrad had died. The heat of that grief was much less intense, the upset now gone. There remained simply a deep sense of loss and sadness. We set off in the car having loaded up a spade, a fork, a couple of rubbish bags and a bottle for getting water. We drove around and picked mum up and headed through Manchester for the cemetery. It was about 12 o'clock when we got there. After a wander around to find the grave I set to, digging over the mess and neatening the edges. The boys ran around as young boys should do and mum stood near chatting and spent time looking for her brother, Uncle Owen's grave. (Owen's story appears later.)

After we finished and had had a look at a number of friends' last resting places, we loaded up the car got the heaters on and headed off towards Manchester. Mum suggested calling in somewhere for a spot of lunch and I fancied 'on the eighth day'. For those of you who are not Mancunian vegetarians, this is a well-known wholefood vegetarian restaurant and shop based in All Saints near to the University and of course hugely popular with students as well as ageing hippies like myself. I drove there without a second thought, parked the car up, and in we went. Mum took one look at the menu which featured such tasty delights as soya and lentil pie, Apple and cheese terrine, and started to mutter on about the food on offer.

I could see she was in a moody and I was in no state to deal with it. She finally agreed to have a cup of tea as there was nothing she could possibly eat even though the counter was filled with delicious food. I got myself and the boys sorted and bought mum a cup of tea which had the 'wrong sort of milk' in. We sat there, the boys and I thoroughly enjoying our meals and mum at odds with the world.

The door opened and two people aged about 60 came in pushing a wheelchair. I assumed it to be a family group; mum, dad and daughter but I don't know why I make that assumption. The young woman in the wheelchair was very physically disabled. Her body was twisted and continually moving (Dyskinetic). Her face was screwed up but you could see that she wore a big smile on her face and was laughing with the two adults on either side of her. We watched her be rolled over to the counter and the complex physical turns she went through to point to this, that and the other that she wanted to eat. Staff from the restaurant clearly knew her and responded accordingly, talking directly to her and not to her parents (as I had assumed the two adults with her to be) and charging her for her food personally. She very cannily accepted the food that she had requested and allowed the others to pay for her. I could see mum watching this from across the restaurant. Then I heard her say to herself "for God's sake what's the matter with me". She turned to me and said "Will you see if there is another baked potato I could have please Ray?" I said of course and went and sorted that out. When I bought the food back and sat down again I asked "what brought that on then?" Mum said "I feel so ashamed of myself fussing about the food when that poor child and her family have so much to deal with and she's smiling and laughing all the time." This from the woman who has been through the things I have described here. I thought it was a mighty approach. It would be lovely never to have to be reminded that there are always those worse off than ourselves. At the very least, such an instant response to that message being brought home by whatever means, has got to be a helpful way of getting through the day. So although I have Parkinson's disease, I don't have a brain tumour, I don't

69

have cancer, I don't have heart failure, I don't live in a war-torn, flooded village and I don't worry where the next meal is coming from. My life could certainly be an awful lot worse.

As Michael J Fox has far more famously said 'I'm a lucky man' in so very many ways that I have no choice really but to face Parkinson's square on and deal with whatever it chooses to throw at me. I will fight clean or dirty for as long as I can. When I know that I am beaten I will give up gracefully and move on to the next stage, where the fighting will begin again. I am likely to get weaker, the bouts might be shorter, the defeat may be more serious or indeed more embarrassing. But the fight will continue on until I reach the point where I cannot function.

Chapter 11 - State support

In broad terms these principles are also applicable to the issue of claiming Disabled Living Allowance (DLA). This is a non-means tested benefit available to people who meet a certain set of criteria around issues of personal care and mobility. Application is by a form which can be completed by the applicant or by someone acting on their behalf. The principle behind this benefit is to assist disabled people with those extra costs created by their disability. As with any benefit, incorrect claims were viewed very dimly and prosecutions would follow if the system decided that the fraud had been deliberate.

As someone who had only once ever applied for benefits before, I was wary of both the process and the documentation. My previous experience had been between the end of my training course in May 1983 and my beginning work as a probation officer in Salford in the October of that year. During that time I claimed the then equivalent of jobseekers allowance and hated it. So I was not minded to claim benefit simply because I was (by my measure) beginning to experience disability. In addition to that, as somebody who earned a reasonable salary, I did not feel that it was appropriate for me to claim or receive a financial benefit. I was not convinced that my level of disability rendered me eligible either. A number of my friends disagreed with me on this point, some of whom were themselves in receipt of this benefit. It was a point raised with me often and one which I found increasingly difficult to argue against. I certainly had plenty of money deducted from my salary each month. I certainly was becoming increasingly disabled, albeit a long way from being wheelchair-bound. The money was there to be given out not to be saved and I would only fill in any such form as honestly as I could so that I would not have any risk of being considered to have committed fraud. In my line of work any such allegation or implication would have serious repercussions and in any event I have some principles.

My friend Jeff has worked with disabled people for many years and himself suffers from a degree of disability. One of the things that he had considerable experience of was applications for Disabled Living Allowance (DLA) and helping people to fill the form in honestly but with more chance of being awarded a payment. Jeff and I had been out of touch for some years, as is often the way of things, but had rekindled our contact via Facebook and met from time to time for lunch and catch up. He had been very surprised when I said I did not receive DLA and the more so when I said I had never applied for it. He was very strongly of the view that if people did not apply for it, it was more likely to suffer in any future cuts. If the party in power at that time said 'look, nobody has applied for it', they are more likely to get rid of it, but if the demand is high that might lead to a higher level of investment. This is another argument I had thought of previously, and it was one that made some sense and we talked for a long time about the whys and wherefores of the benefit and my eligibility or otherwise to receive it. Jeff was very capable in formulating a strong case as to why I should apply and generously offered to help me in completing the form if I wished. Not being one to reinvent wheels unnecessarily I took him up on his offer and made a phone call to the relevant number to request a copy of the form. The very helpful woman who answered explained to me that the clock started at that point and that if I were to be awarded a payment it would be backdated to this date and time. She also underlined the fact that there were deadlines for the completion and return of the form as well as for the stages in the process and asked that I ensure that I met my responsibility in delivering the form properly and fully completed and on time.

One's conscience can often lead to imagined views of others. I had expected to have more of a challenging conversation with somebody who assumed I was cheating. I came off the phone feeling very positively encouraged. Strange the way things can turn round.

The form arrived a few days later. The supporting notes had quite properly been written in language that was designed to be accessible to those perhaps less experienced in the completion of official forms but even so, the form looked complex on first scrutiny.

Jeff's general advice to me in case I chose not to involve him in the completion of the form had been to ensure that I answered every question based on the worst scenario or worst day or worst level of functioning that I had experienced. Advice? Sound and simple. Application of said advice? Hugely difficult!

One of the realities of Parkinson's is its variability. This applies in terms of person to person as well as from stage to stage of the condition overall. Indeed the effect of the condition varies from day to day and hour to hour according to stress and medication levels and so on. This means that on any given day at any given time I might be able to do something or not.

Whilst the form invites you to describe how your condition affects you, this of course can be hugely difficult to get right. For example the form asks a question about how far you can walk, or for how long before you experience severe discomfort or shortness of breath. Now on some days I can walk for 3 or 4 miles, albeit with a stick and taking it easy. On other days I wouldn't feel able to walk any particular distance even a half mile down to town. I often get breathless but to some extent that depends whether I go up or down hill when I leave the house. The form asks you to say that in less than 100 metres you experience severe discomfort and/or breathlessness. This might happen to you on a day when you happen to go out very early, before your medicine kicked in and never happen if you wait until half an hour after you have taken them. People who are fighting their condition and its effects find it very challenging to describe themselves as unable to walk 100 m without suffering severe discomfort. It would be as if one was admitting to being more disabled than one was, even though it would be absolutely true to say that there were circumstances in which this low level of functioning applied. Many people would simply respond 'not applicable' to the question and move on, this of course allowing the Assessor to assert that mobility was not an issue.

So it is that completing the form proves to be a difficult task. I want to be able to write that I do have difficulty walking and I want to go on to quantify it both pre-and post-medication but I can't. I do my best and make it clear that I am describing my worst day and the worst time of day and therefore my worst level of functioning.

The form covers a series of areas of life. Cooking and cleaning; self-care; toileting and so forth. I described how I can no longer carry two drinks from the kitchen into the living room in one journey. I described how, if my hands were shaking badly I would struggle to chop vegetables. Equally, when steady and medicated I can cut them perfectly well. With Jeff's constant reminders and encouragement I managed to answer all the questions in a way that I judged to be honest as well as accurately describing my worst state. It took half a day and by the end of that time my sense of myself was fairly low. I'd described myself as being the worst of everything in terms of physical functioning. It was a surprise to me a few weeks later to receive a letter from DLA confirming that they had allocated me the lowest level of care but no mobility award. I was rather surprised until I was told that the answer lies in the fact that one of the tests for the care side is one's ability to safely to prepare a meal. However this doesn't mean any meal. It means a particular meal and it would be the case that at my worst I would struggle to manage that particular task. It felt like I was admitting that I couldn't feed myself. However that was the basis of the award that was given. Jeff and others thought I should appeal against the decision about mobility but I could not bring myself to do so for all the reasons that I have described and because I found the whole process immensely difficult emotionally.

It was probably two or three years later, in about 2009, that I had cause to contact the local Parkinson's UK welfare worker. I wanted some advice on adjustments at work legislation in order to be up-to-date with what might be possible to help me stay working.

Danny was a livewire. He had worked in the forces as a welfare officer as well as being a trained soldier. He was energetic, personable, bright and very thorough. As we discussed reasonable adjustments and other issues he asked about my DLA. When I told him what I received he said that in his view I would be eligible for more and that I should consider reapplying and letting him fill the form in. We went through the issues of the honesty of the answers and he was very helpful in the way that he described his approach. He was willing to complete the form for me, with me being there answering his questions. He would deal with the issue of describing what 'the worst' is like and check it with me before putting it down as my response. This sounded worth a go so we arranged for him to come back in a few weeks' time. He arrived quite early, before the boys had left for school and we were all chatting, whilst I was making brews, gathering documents and so forth. As I carried his tea the short distance from the kettle to the table, I experienced one of my early 'sticky foot' episodes. Half his tea went on the floor. I cursed. Dot calmly ushered me out of the kitchen and set about cleaning up and making another brew. I could see Danny taking all of this in and sure enough, as the day went on he made reference to that and asked a number of questions about my experiences of getting stuck, carrying and so forth.

Sticky foot is a symptom of Parkinson's which, like all other symptoms is not experienced by everybody with the condition. It is a fairly literal description. When wanting to initiate movement, such as stepping back from the sink after washing hands, the feet stay firmly planted on the floor, whilst the rest of the body begins to move. The other common occurrence happens on walking through doorways. As you get to the doorway the feet stop moving without any announcement of their intention. As I'm sure you can imagine, this leads to falls. One of the ways of managing walking through doors safely is to count and walk to the beat. A strong beat or rhythmic piece of music somehow gives a person with Parkinson's control back over these peculiar happenings.

They say the proof of the pudding is in the eating and sure enough within a fortnight the answer came back from the DLA that I had been awarded the highest level of mobility along with the lower level of care. Whilst it is true that I had deteriorated over the two years, it was in my opinion slight deterioration. However with the detail that he was able to put in the document, he was able to meet the criteria without me feeling in any way that I had padded my experiences.

It's important I think, to acknowledge that DLA is a tremendous benefit for people with disability. It can be paid irrespective of your circumstances, your salary or any other income that comes into the household or your savings. Having the upper level of mobility makes you eligible to lease a Motability vehicle having your money paid directly to Motability and thus being able to take advantage of a superb package of care and support in vehicle ownership. This again is an excellent benefit which allows me to have a new car every three years which is taxed and insured and serviced for that period of time after which I am entitled to change it. As the DLA for this scheme is paid directly from the Works and Benefits section to the car provider I don't miss the money in the sense of having to receive it and then pay it over. It also means that a recipient can't get into debt with this arrangement which is also important. All that has to be paid for is fuel. People are even allowed to have an additional driver named on the insurance policy. It really is a tremendous scheme. When the engine on my first car blew up on the M1 on a dark winter's night in Yorkshire, I was home at midnight in another rental vehicle and my car was already in the garage to be fixed.

Chapter 12 - Falling

As I write this in 2016, 21 years after diagnosis and having turned 60 (so it says on my birth Certificate, but my maths is poor and I cannot make the numbers add up to 60 at all), I know such a lot about Parkinson's and its effects, which are insidious, variable and vicious. I know much of what is yet to come and what I may have to deal with. My family know a lot more than they did and many of them are still struggling to understand the details and some of the effects on me and the consequences of those effects in terms of my attitudes and behaviours.

A considerable amount of this learning has come in the last four years. For much of the time since diagnosis, I have lived with Parkinson's as a condition which I knew I had, and for which I took medication but which in all honesty had very little limiting effect that I was prepared to acknowledge. I have had some difficulties with side-effects from medication, but felt little impact on my general ability, my cognition, and my capacity to undertake my work or to get on with life in a perfectly normal manner. The last six years however have introduced visible changes to my walking, my posture, I leak out of the right-hand corner of my mouth. My confidence became shredded. Occasionally, I fall down.

There are two sides to falling down which are problematic. One of course is hurting oneself and there is the potential to do serious harm. The other is public reaction to and perception of somebody who falls down for no apparent reason. All in all, I have fallen about a dozen times in the last few years and I have been extremely fortunate not to hurt myself too badly. I have never required medical treatment for a fall and I've never banged my head, although I am continually anxious about falling backwards and doing so. Several of the falls have been in the house and should anyone be about they will hear me roundly cursing myself and my stupid condition. But that's about all they would hear. I can get myself up the correct way (as advised by physiotherapist anyway) and I can brush myself off and start all over again quite happily.

Whilst at work I was travelling one day to Newcastle by train. I had to change at York and my train from Manchester was running a little late so the time available for me to catch my booked train was fairly tight. I was wearing a suit, shirt and tie et cetera pulling a suitcase with a week's worth of personal kit and carrying a heavy laptop in a shoulder bag. I disembarked the train quite far down the platform. In York station, to change platform one has to go towards the exit of the building where the stairs will carry you to the platform required. Because I have a distance to go and was very aware (and a little anxious about) the tight timeframe I started to jog along the platform. The next thing I knew I was falling I have let go of my personal luggage and the laptop was heading towards the floor. I managed to get my hands out and down and thus avoid full-face contact with the concrete.

I was little shocked but managed not to swear too loudly. I did a quick inventory for sources of pain, torn clothing et cetera before moving. I got myself up, checked that my trouser knees weren't torn, nor the backside ripped and noted one or two people staring at me from the trains standing at the nearby platforms. I can understand why people think that people with Parkinson's are drunk, but I wish they wouldn't leap to this as their first assumption. I'm sure if I had stayed prone or shouted for help somebody would have come, first aiders from the station staff at the very least. But as I stood there collecting my bags along with my thoughts and my spilled emotions I noted that nobody made a move to offer assistance. Something to think about.

I thought about this a lot for the next few weeks. The significance of falling is well worth thinking about. It is made clear that Parkinson's does not kill you. It does however make a person more vulnerable and leaves them with reduced personal resources, to deal with, for example pneumonia or a cracked skull. So an injury or infection, which requires fighting has a greater chance of winning than of being defeated as far as people with Parkinsons are concerned. As one who's balance is effected whereas my voice (as an example of the individuality of Parkinsons) is relatively untouched, I found myself back in the mind-set of writing creatively about that which I had been pondering and penned the following, brushing it up over a period of a few weeks. Nothing much has joined it however, so instead of making a second collection, it stands alone, hence including it here.

Fear of Falling (with a nod to David Bowie & Dylan Thomas)

An autumn day, 2012, I'm waiting for a fall.
not a fall from grace, reputation mocked,
shame spread thick as manure;
but a real fall, a hard knock,
consequences far more painful to endure.

Clinging to the doorjamb, my faith in its plumb-líke stability given lie
by my unintended efforts to rip it from its roots.
Surveying the once familiar room-scape, its cosiness turned to threat,
lying in wait for me when I plunge headlong,
to the place only my feet should tread.

The day will come, the threat ever-present as the sun.
Sometimes I visualise in slow motion, falling gracefully in error,
bouncing gently off thrusting IKEA crags,
landing, softly on carpet inches thick,
climbing back up, laughing, crowing at my vanquishing of the terror.

But of late, my almost fun daydream has turned harsh;
slow motion and bouncing, replaced by speed and crashing,
gently now as broken as bones on the oak table,
when fast-flying object meets unmoving mass;
a no-brainer in more ways than one.

My brain, lost in space, in overdrive and panicking
will throw on the aptly named dead man's brake,
when my body misbehaves
and acts without permission.
Its "ground control to Major Tom, your circuit's dead - so STOP!"

There is a constant in physics
that speed = distance over time

But I wouldn't have time to work out the speed with which my
nose describes a parabola
that ends at the first obstruction.
Then it's brakes and breaks together.

Like Morecambe and Wise, or Penn and Teller
Parkinson's and Falling just go together.
So where's the laugh to fit the tease?
It's in the arms and legs,
never being at ease.

But I will not go gentle into this first fall,
And I shall rage against this damned condition.
I will burn PD with my loudest voice
And curse its degenerative, progressive imposition.

Chapter 13 - The Tyranny of Tablets

So I reached a point in the autumn of 1995 when I had just turned 40. Bizarrely, I was relieved to have got past 39, the age at which my dad died. (I say bizarrely, but a few years later, in a conversation with my brother, Paul, he said that he was worried about exactly the same issue, and was relieved when he did so). I was in the prime of my life really, with a growing family of dependents, lots of career opportunities and considerable potential ahead. I also went around with a degenerative neurological disease about which I still knew relatively little. My family all knew I had it and, like me, none of them really understood it or were aware of what was likely to happen over the coming years.

I know that Dot worries about me and feels a sense of responsibility. For me, she is my wife not my carer but I'm also not so stupid that I don't realise that there is a blur between the two roles. My job is to make sure that blurred area is as narrow as possible without being unrealistic.

I know that my two sons worry about me and I hate that and I love that. They should be free from concerns about my health and not be having to even contemplate caring arrangements or any such nonsense. I know full well that they are not alone in this and that many young men and women have disabled parents who have additional needs. I am keen to keep any such additional needs to myself where possible and certainly not to allow them to impact on my boys' or their wives' lives. Equally however I know that it is an indication of their love and respect for me and I cannot value that highly enough.

At the end of July 2010 I went off sick and my doctor diagnosed depression. This was my third episode of depression. I was prescribed a new sort of antidepressant and took two weeks off work, fully expecting to return thereafter to my normal workload. The horrible realisation during that two weeks that I needed more time off led to lots of discussion with my line manager. I began to realise that I was no longer fit to do my job. This was an extremely difficult discovery to handle and it took considerable time and not a little support from a range of people for me to work through. In June 2011 I was officially retired from work and given my full pension. I would be lying if I did not admit that I am much less stressed now and adjusting to this stage of my life reasonably well in the circumstances. However, I'm rushing ahead so we'll get back to the theme of this chapter and come back to the detail of the ending of my career a little later.

The major treatment for Parkinson's is drug based. There is a range of medications to treat symptoms which can be useful for early-onset, particularly where the symptoms are relatively mild. There is a school of thought that this can slow down the progress of the condition, thus delaying the time when dopamine replacement therapy becomes necessary. My Parkinson's was early-onset and my symptoms were mild and so I was treated with a drug called Trihexyphenidyl. This was meant to alleviate symptoms, particularly tremor.

I have to admit that I was scared by the prospect of taking what I judged to be powerful medication for the rest of my life. They would affect liver and kidneys never mind the brain and the blood brain barrier itself. Of course, academically, one can assess that it is a balancing act of lifestyle and relative freedom, at the cost of taking the drugs. I was unsure to what extent I might experience side effects, but the list in the patient information leaflet was ominous as far as I was concerned. I certainly didn't want to be trying to work and handling any bad effects and so I decided that I would wait until the February half term holiday when we had booked to go away to a beautiful campsite, in the Trossachs in Scotland. If that sounds a bit contradictory as well as cold and wet please don't be misled. This was a campsite with about 16 very attractive log cabins, placed so that none overlooked another, on the shallow banks of Loch Lubnaig, a short drive north of Calender, home of the world-famous Dr Finlay's casebook and the slightly less famous, but far more interesting to the children, pancake shop.

I figured that here I could take some time out to myself whilst the boys were out playing and Dot with friends. I could go through whatever difficulties I would have to go through with medication without being seen by others to go through any difficult side-effects. One of the most common side effects of many drugs is nausea and sickness. I tend to a weak stomach in that respect, so if there's a prospect of vomiting, there's a high likelihood of me joining in...noisily, because one can't help it. And it isn't pleasant for the afflicted to know that others can hear or see, never mind how it is for anyone visiting at the time.

The day dawned. D-Day! Drug day! I had been prescribed to start with just one per day and work my way up over a period of three weeks to 3 per day. This process is called titration and is designed to help minimise side effects and enable the body to habituate itself to a new chemical gradually. I had decided to start with the lunchtime tablet and then on the second week to introduce the evening one and on the third the breakfast dose. Furthermore, I had decided to start my new habit on the Tuesday. Tuesday meant that I had a couple of days of carefree holiday after the long drive and four days to find out exactly what the medication might do to me when I took it so that I could make preparations for the homeward journey as required. Like so many drugs, there is a caution with trihexyphenidyl about using machinery or driving if the medication causes drowsiness.

We had lunch as usual and the boys got their boots on and went to find their friends around the site. Dot looked at me with a questioning look and went over to Pauline and Al's cabin for an early wine or whiskey disguised as a mug of tea. I made myself a genuine mug of tea (my version of panacea) got a glass of water and the bottle of pills and sat down on the settee. An observer would have thought perhaps that these were preparations for a suicide without the note. The participant himself might have felt that way a little, albeit without the intent. At two o'clock I screwed off the white plastic lid which required that you press it down before you turn it, and tipped one small white tablet into the palm of my right hand. I closed my ring finger over it and screwed the top back on the bottle of tablets with my thumb and forefinger. I sat down and leaned back and reached out my left hand for the glass of water. I put the tablet on my tongue, drank the whole tumbler, and washed the poison pill down my throat feeling it hit the top of the stomach along with the swallow of water. Then simply knowing that it was inside me, I put my feet lengthways on the settee and thought I would wait and see what would happen.

I lay there and probably dozed a little for 20 to 25 minutes. I came to and sat up allowing my mind to focus itself on different parts of my body, heart, stomach, limbs, brain. I was aware of ... absolutely no effect whatsoever. I may as well have taken a deep breath for the effect that was noticeable from the tablet. I felt a sense of relief and let down at the same time. This was supposedly powerful medication. The leaflet in the package carried all sorts of warnings and cautions and it was supposed to affect my brain. Where was the effect? At the same time I was so relieved that I was still alive and feeling no ill effects that I began to think that may be this new life wouldn't be as bad as I had imagined. Limited judgements from limited information.

So, as directed, I slowly built up the dosage to the required level. All the time in those few weeks waiting for some impact or sensation that I could identify as different than normal. It never came. Were they doing me any good? How would I know? I read up about them. Possibly they slow down the progress of the condition. Can't measure that. So, here I was taking drugs on a regular basis that were affecting my brain but I had no idea if they were doing me any good or indeed any harm.

I stayed on Trihexyphenidyl for several years. Eventually I began to see evidence of its insidious hold over me. There are two stories that illustrate this. One of them is inconsequential and amusing. The other was horribly embarrassing and indicative of things to come.

I pulled into the car park at the Tesco in Baguely near to where my mum lives. I was on my way to visit her and had promised to buy some soup and other groceries that she needed as my sister, who usually did her shopping, was away. This particular store is always very busy and the car park very crowded. I tend to park away from the store door as most people seem to want to park in the entrance hall or as near as possible after that.

I got out of the car, shut the door and locked it. I had a quick scan around to identify the area of the car park that it was in - B3. I walked carefully along the rows of parked cars avoiding those moving out of their space having finished their shopping and those who were pulling into the empty spaces as near as possible to the door to go and get theirs. I wandered around the store filling a basket with mum's groceries and having a look at the flat panel TVs. This all took a good 10 minutes after which I joined a queue on a till and wasted a good 10 minutes.

I walked out, a carrier bag in each hand and glanced around the car park and headed for area B3. When I got there I went to the space where I was sure I had parked. It was close to one of the shelters for the shopping trolleys which was one of the things I used to mark the place in my mind. My car was not amongst those parked there. My stomach was immediately clutched with the anxiety of fearing that the car has been stolen. I quickly thought back. Did I lock it? Yes I am absolutely sure I did. Was there anything left on the back seat that might entice a thief? No I don't believe so. Since I worked as a car crime prevention officer in Salford, I have taken to heart the lessons I gave to others and didn't leave things lying around in the car. Damnit, I must be on the wrong row. I walked across to the rows behind but was sure that wasn't where I had been. Nevertheless, I did look intently at the cars parked near to the trolley shelter. Mine wasn't there. B3; I was sure that was where I had parked. Taking a deep breath to quell the anxiety now raging in my stomach I try to summons my confidence that I did know where I had parked the car and I walked back to the trolley shelter in area B3. I stood up on the kerb so that I could get a slightly better look. I scanned up and down the rows but could not see my silver Honda Accord. This was the car to surpass all the others I have owned. Automatic to accommodate my loss of control of my left leg when trying to use a clutch, especially for fine manoeuvring. Well engineered and comfortable all day long. Dammit - if it was gone, I would be really stuck.

I decided to telephone my eldest son, Matthew. A sensible man plus he could come and get me if the car really was gone. As I was explaining my dilemma to him, I looked at the car that was in the space where I thought I had parked. It was my number plate. It was my car. I had stood next to it, walked past it five or six times in the last five minutes. I have been actively looking for it and had not seen it right under my nose in the place I thought it was. I thanked Matt for listening and I could tell that he wondered what was going on. So did I. Okay I had worked a full day and had been busy, but still it wasn't yet eight o'clock at night. It was summertime the sky was bright. No, I couldn't understand it. I sat in the car to gather my thoughts. A little bell tinkled away in the far distant recesses of my mind; 'can affect cognition'. That was written in the papers of at least some of the drugs I took and I'm sure it was the Trihexyphenidyl. I would have to look into this a

90

little more. Nothing like it had happened before. I hoped now that it would not happen again.

So that was an event which was of no consequence and which has become one of those little stories in family life that gets referenced from time to time and only those of us who know about it get the reference and fall about laughing at my inability to see my own car. The other incident embarrassed me tremendously and raised much more serious issues. What these two things have in common is that I can say that both of them were the result of long-term use of Trihexyphenidyl.

It was a hot, sunny Thursday afternoon in September. I was walking from Ipswich railway station towards a glass monolith which is their civic centre. It had been built by a private insurance company in the style that private insurance companies build buildings to work as their headquarters. Clean, sharp edged and glass, lots and lots of dark glass. Inside, an atrium, and the middle of the building completely empty with balconies hanging from each floor with a variety of functions; cafes, information services, security and so forth. Beyond each balcony were the open plan offices for the majority of staff and beyond them again toward the outer wall of the building, offices for senior staff.

I was there to attend a meeting in the office of the most senior of senior officers, that of the chief executive. He was the chair of the Youth Offending Team Management Board and was therefore the person responsible for ensuring that the changes to be made following my inspection of that service did actually happen. This was a meeting to inform the management board exactly what my judgements were of their youth offending service and some direction as to what needed to be done to bring about ongoing improvement.

I loved my job. As one of Her Majesty's Inspectors of Probation I enjoyed a reasonably senior position within the criminal justice system, where I had worked my whole adult life. This post was built on the back of many years of experience in the field as a community service supervisor, then officer, qualified probation officer, senior probation officer and district manager. I had also spent three years working as a project manager at the Home Office on the national probation service information system. I had run various teams with specialist functions as well as generic operations, I had run one of the biggest probation and bail hostels in the country, I have headed a district-based service (which was the best job I have ever had) comprising over 90 staff and a budget of £3m pa with some 14,000 cases under supervision and I reckon that I knew pretty much all there was to know about what went on in the probation service. In 2002, I took off my poacher's jumper and donned my gamekeeper's cap. It was always fun on arrival for a first contact with the service to check just how long it took for somebody to try, subtly or otherwise, to find out whether I was a grey suit from the Ministry or someone who knew what he was talking about. It was always fun to explain that I was both and was good at both roles. People tended not to challenge so much once they recognised the experience that I had.

I walked up the steps of the Civic Centre, through the swing doors and presented myself at the security desk. I explained who I was and showed my ID. The chief exec's PA was immediately summonsed to come and show me into his office.

This was the usual response we got in places like this and it suited me very well, saving a lot of messing about and waiting. I was shown into the room and the chief executive saw me immediately and smiling broadly walked over to me with his hand extended. We shook warmly having met a couple of times during the inspection process and he attended to making coffee and getting me settled in the appropriate seat. Also present was the director of children's services, the director of education, the assistant chief constable, the head of the primary care trust and one or two other notables. This was the level at which I operated and I recognised the importance of getting my part of that process right. I took my job seriously and as much as I could enjoy a joke and a laugh during the inspection process there were times to be serious: this meeting was one of them although not because there was any bad news to be delivered. The service was well run and was doing a lot of good work, but there were things to be improved upon. That mattered and needed to be attended to carefully and thoroughly.

I had prepared a PowerPoint presentation and asked for a projector to be available to which I could connect my laptop. Unfortunately part of the message didn't get through to somewhere and nothing was available. Ever resourceful however, I had of course brought a number of paper copies in different formats and we agreed which version would be copied off for all members of the meeting. One of the administrators was duly dispatched to attend to that and there was a general shuffling of bums in seats and a refilling of coffee cups whilst that business went on.

Eventually the copies of my presentation re-appeared and were duly distributed. I had put the presentation together using our standard template which we had created to ensure that we all presented more or less the same issues at these feedback meetings. I had amended it of course, as it was rather clumsy in part and I tended to work the messages that I wanted to give into four or five small hand-held cards each with a headline on. I would take the time to learn what was related to the headline but speak to that without notes to avoid the appearance of reading out a script. It was a skill I had developed over the years and one at which I was fairly competent.

The meeting got under way and my item was the first substantive one. I set about my presentation wrapping it in the congratulatory tones of a well-organised inspection by a good, high performing service. I started then to work my way through the headline issues in front of this group of people who would be allocating resources whether they liked it or not based on what I said at this juncture. The next thing I knew I was looking across the table at a number of faces one or two of which were slightly puzzled and I had not got the faintest clue what I just said. My cards were down on the table and I didn't know what I had just read from a card or what I could see out of the window. I was shocked and all I could think was "pull yourself together, pull yourself together. Get on with it and get back on track and get this job done". After another moment I realised absolutely that I simply did not know where I was up to in the presentation or what I had covered. This left me with no option but to pick a point in the presentation and go forward from there.

I delivered the rest of the information steadily and reasonably and invited questions at the end. To my great relief there were very few and none from the puzzled faces that sat across from me. Once the questions had finished, the chair made a vote of thanks without any reference to my hiatus in the middle of this meeting. I packed my bags, wished them all well and left quickly. I was mortified. What was worse I thought, was that I didn't know what had happened.

Chapter 14 - Dopamine Agonists

In recent years there has been considerable interest in the category of medication known as dopamine agonists. These are designed to extend the useful period of time that dopamine is available within the brain by preventing it from being neutralised by other chemicals it comes across (That's a very basic explanation. For more technical information please Google dopamine agonists, side-effects).

There have been many accounts of these tablets causing changes of personality, turning people into apparent monsters, leaving spouses, gambling away life savings, becoming sex addicts. All these things have happened and may have been caused by the person concerned taking dopamine agonist medication. Equally however it is true to say that many people who take dopamine agonists do not do those things. A lot of them of them may have slight leanings toward one or the other habits which may or may not be enhanced by the effect of the relevant medication. There is also some evidence that people using dopamine agonists may slip into obsessive/compulsive behaviours. If you count those on whom there is a mild and non-problematic side effect it may be a substantial minority. But for the vast majority, this medication is beneficial for their Parkinson's symptoms.

I think a lot of the difficulty over this issue is due to the climate of fear that exists around the health service and the pharmaceutical industry about people suing them. There seems to be a genuine anxiety that admitting a mistake or a consequence that is negative by whatever measure will result in punitive action being taken. This makes it difficult for neurologists properly to monitor the effects on those using dopamine agonists. This in turn is compounded by the reality that until things become a catastrophe, much of the behaviour that may be being prompted by these medications is very pleasurable and users have no desire to stop taking them and so losing the enjoyment of the "side-effect". This in turn is likely to prevent the Person with Parkinson's from being entirely honest about the extent of or consequences from, any such behaviour. Obviously, once things hit the wall or go too far this is a different matter. It would have been ideal to have more open and exploratory conversations between neurologists and patients which might shed a lot more light on this particular problem. As it stands, I think doctors will be very cautious in exploring the issues and even if they do probe, the patient may well not be forthcoming.

I was put on a dopamine agonist (DA) tablet after about six years. My tremor had worsened and I was displaying other symptoms which frankly I did not like. I was beginning to feel a little tired and did not like the way that the Trihexyphenidyl was affecting my thinking. I was taken off that and put on the DA. I was still worried about taking this medication. I was anxious about coming off one and going on to another and getting the timing of that right. I was worried about the side-effects of the DA having read the patient information leaflet within the box that the tablets came in. Also I had read on various Internet forums for people with Parkinson's about some of the cases of extreme changes of personality and I was worried about that. My experience with Trihexyphenidyl had been relatively mild but did not provide a good lead-in to any other medication at all. My expectations of difficulty were high.

As before, I titrated, starting with half a tablet and building up over four or five weeks to three tablets a day. These made me feel rough, groggy and it was difficult to tell whether they had any beneficial effect on my tremor. But I persevered mainly because I didn't know what else I should do. I had been on three DAs daily for about eight months when I was away again in Suffolk on an inspection. I was leading the inspection and it was the last but one day. We were staying in a hotel in the centre of town and I had come back from my day's meetings at the probation area's headquarters feeling a little peculiar.

As the evening went on I felt less and less well, as if I was suffering from a virus. I went to bed early and got very hot and felt very restless. This was not anything new but it was difficult to allocate cause-and-effect. At seven o'clock the following morning I felt quite woozy but got up and dressed and went down to breakfast in any event. It was the last day of the inspection, we had to check out of the hotel that morning and I had several commitments from nine o'clock until two in the afternoon. Two colleagues were seated near the entrance to the restaurant and as I walked in there was a shocked look on their faces. They asked me what the matter was. I commented that I didn't feel particularly well but I would manage and we should carry on as planned. They looked doubtful, but I was lead inspector so they accepted what I said. Half an hour later, having eaten, I knew that there was no way I was going to manage an inspection today nor a journey home. I walked back to my colleagues sweating profusely and feeling very hot. Before I could say anything they both said to me that I looked awful and was not to be thinking about working today. This time I agreed with them.

We arranged for them to cover what needed covering and cancel what could be cancelled. I went back to my room and called the office to report my condition and to ask that my admin support worker extend my stay in the hotel. I rang home again to explain what was happening took a couple of paracetamol and climbed into bed. I stayed there for the whole day dozing, waking, dozing and waking. Two colleagues knocked on the door at different times of the day to check that I was okay. I knew they had come back specially to do that but we just pretended that they were passing and I thanked them and just asked them to carry on as best they could and that I would look after myself and be fine. Later on that night I still felt far from well. I had remained in bed the whole day and did not really feel much better. I dosed with paracetamol several times and had become aware of a dull ache in my right forearm. I awoke finally at about 2 am. I did a self check and decided I felt somewhat better and that now was a good time to go as the roads would be empty of traffic and I would get a quick run up the M1. This is a four-hour journey at a minimum so I don't know why I thought it would be a quick run. I packed my bags and work backpack. I got the night manager and explained what had been going on and he confirmed that with his paperwork. I paid the bill and my suitcase and backpack were put in the boot. It was by now 3 am. I set the satellite navigation unit for home and followed its instructions through Ipswich until I was heading out to the A 14. Because it was midsummer, it was becoming light slowly and certainly by 3:45 it was sufficiently light to see to drive without headlights. I had a short sleeved shirt on, and as the daylight increased in intensity I noticed faint red lines on my right forearm around where the throbbing had been. I had not seen these before, didn't know what they were and wasn't too happy about them.

The drive home required two stops to gather myself, use the loo, drink coffee and eat something. I finally got in at 9 am. By now my right forearm was throbbing again and I looked at it and I could see that it was beginning to swell around the wrist. The back of the hand was podgy and the red thread veins as I referred to them seemed longer. I couldn't think what else to do so I took myself off to bed again. I assumed I had a virus that would pass the way viruses do with warmth, sleep and hot drinks. The following day, I woke up to find that my right arm was double its size, very painful and a frightful sight. I made an appointment immediately with my GP for that evening.

I wore a long-sleeved jacket and as I was explaining to him what the problem was he said "let's have a look then". I carefully removed my jacket and was taken aback to hear the Dr's "Oooh".
"Shit" I thought. "If he thinks it looks bad I'm really bothered now". "Well, what do you think it is?" I asked.
"I'm not sure at the moment" he replied "let me take a closer look". With that he took out a small eyepiece with a thick lens and had a very close examination of the red thread lines. He asked one or two questions about how things had come about then looked up one of his textbooks.
"Hhmmm. I think you have a case of vasculitis. This is usually an allergic reaction to medication and from what I can tell it's probably your dopamine agonist. You haven't felt great on it all the time you've been having it. The treatment is to take you off that medication immediately. I know that's not the way

that you should come off it but I think it's what we have to do. I'll prescribe you the other main DA drug- it's called Pramipexole or Mirapexin, so you will have the chance of some benefit for your Parkinson's symptoms. I'm going to sign you off two weeks and you must rest and be careful. If you get any worse you need to come straight back but I think you will find that it doesn't get worse and after a few days will start to heal and reduce. Take paracetemol for the pain and I'll see you in a fortnight in any event."

Before I left I asked him whether vasculitis was a condition about which we should be concerned. He explained that it can appear anywhere in the body as it is an infection of the bloodstream. He made the point that had it occurred in one of my main organs internally I would have had no idea that it was there until it had done its damage. By happening in my forearm it allowed me to see what was going on and therefore to respond more quickly. My arm was a frightful mess and not to be shown in public as far as I was concerned.

I was off for the full two weeks and even when I returned to work I still had swollen parts of my arm which had turned purple as part of the healing process. It looked like it had been battered with sticks. The fact that this happened with a dopamine agonist doesn't mean that this is to be viewed as a possible side effect like character change that was described earlier. This just happened to be my reaction to a particular medication. As with so many things in this tale, it could have been a lot worse.

Chapter 15 – Children's Needs

There's a lot written and discussed about telling children bad news or difficult messages. There are variations according to age, numbers of children in the family, whereabouts in the sequence a child is. I'm sure there are many other factors that people could try to take into account to make sure that they delivered the message as well as possible so that it was the least damaging to the child. This is surely, as a minimum on the face of it, what we would all want. But what does it mean? 'The least damaging'. Some things are facts of life. We treat them differently at our peril, I believe. Some facts of life are very difficult and painful but they are nonetheless facts of life. So sometimes we may worry about and seek to minimise the 'damage' to a child right now and in so doing cause difficulties for them later in life when they are facing the actuality of some of the difficult things that life invariably brings us.

So, I had to tell my boys about Parkinson's. It was never going to be stress-free, but it was not the hardest thing I had had to tell them about. I'm not going to pretend here that I think these are easy issues and I'm certainly not going to assert that the way I handled them was the right way. I wouldn't recommend any way to anybody to tell their children bad news. I think that every family has its way of doing things and has to live with the consequences good, bad or indifferent. Above all, the child needs to know that he or she is loved by and safe with, whoever is with them.

I have no recollection of my dad and I certainly don't recall his death or being told that he had died. I know that mum, in her distress, having to tell us something, told me at least, no doubt trying to protect me to a degree and with all good intentions that God had taken him to heaven. I know I wasn't allowed to go to the funeral but I have no memory of wanting to, or of me having any understanding of what was going on around me at that time. Apparently, about 18 months after his death I turned to my mum and said "I don't like God". For a 4 1/2 year old Polish/Irish/Catholic boy, that was quite a statement, indicative perhaps of things to come. Anyway I was asked the reason for this new position on the deity. My answer was based entirely on what I had been told. It was completely logical, simple and straightforward: "because he won't let my daddy come home".

Mum has told me that my logic floored her completely. She could not understand why she had not seen what a small child would make of the messages she had given. In trying to give me a positive slant she had raised doubts in my mind completely unintentionally. So, I am aware that many adults explain death to children in a variety of ways. Gone with the angels; to be with grandma: In the clouds: these are just some of the things that I know people have told children about a death. Just for myself I have to say that I think the honest, straightforward, blunt and above all, short answer is best. Children ask a question such as "where do babies come from?" Some folk worry that this requires an encyclopaedic answer. They then enter into a lengthy account of relationships, legality, love and sexuality and so forth, when the answer that will satisfy the child at the point at which the question is asked is, "from mummy's tummy". The next question "how does the baby get in there?" comes later and requires that slightly more sophisticated answer as befits a later developmental stage.

So it was in the relatively early hours of 7th August 1989 that I was faced with the prospect of gathering together my two small sons, aged six and eight and telling them that their little brother had died during his birth. We had spent months preparing them for his arrival. They had both made woolly balls for him to play with and joined in with us setting up a Moses basket and picking out various items for his first few days in our family. I had explained what would happen. They would go to Cynthia's house, a regular visiting point for the whole family and where they felt completely at home. We would go to hospital and the baby would be born and I would come back and get them and take them to see him (or her, we did not know beforehand) so they could say hello before we all went home.

I parked my car in Cynthia's drive. The lump of lead in the pit of my stomach became twice as heavy. It was 7:30 in the morning of what had been the worst night of my life. There was no way to avoid what was to come. I knocked at the door and heard the sound of excited voices, egged on by happy adults running down the hallway to answer me. The door swung open and I was faced with Cynthia and Alan and my two boys in front of them. Cynthia and Alan took one look at my face and both of them took a step backwards. I stepped in putting an arm round each of the boys and pulling them close to me. I asked Alan if I could use their bedroom for a few minutes, as it was the first room along the corridor. He nodded. I took the boys in to the bedroom. They had gone quiet now. They could pick up my mood if not understand it. I sat on the edge of the bed and arm round each of them and pulled them right in close to my chest. "I'm so sorry" I said "you had a little brother tonight but he was very poorly and the doctors couldn't make him better and he died." I held on to them tightly for several minutes, during which time there were a few little questions, though I cannot recall the detail. Then I took them each by the hand and led them through to the living room. Cynthia had the tea brewed and drinks and biscuits for the boys and she took them off me and distracted them with sweets and playthings. Alan walked over and held me, something he'd never done before and which didn't come easily to him, but it was no time for playing men. I stood in silence drinking my tea. After a while Cynthia came and joined us as the boys played with their friends. I noticed Matthew crying and went over and chatted to him for a little while. He didn't have any questions, he was just upset and I just comforted him as best I could. There's no magic secret to this. A little one feeling upset being held close by a loving parent is going to begin to feel safer in terms of their immediate concerns. That doesn't mean that there's not going to be lots of tears and upset in the days to come. They will have to be addressed at the time and there is little point in trying to head it off because it needs to be gone through for a healthy resolution to be achieved. This is the grieving process. It is not an event or one-of occurrence and it is applicable in many circumstances. After a while Matthew settled and seemed content enough to play with the others so I went back to join my friends and to tell them the sorry story.

So, in our case, telling my children who by then were aged 12 and 11 that I had Parkinson's disease, was far from the worst thing I had ever had to do. They had been aware that I had been going to the hospital because I had this peculiar tremor. It was more a matter of confirmation than information. Telling them the name of the condition I had and a few basic universal facts about it was sufficient at the time. Over the coming months there were discussions around the tea table, questions directly to one or other of us, and the reading of leaflets and pamphlets that I picked up at various places. Both boys felt quite confident and comfortable to ask questions of both Dot and I, which I found a very positive sign. They were clear that this wasn't an illness that was going to kill me and indeed it wasn't many weeks before the jokes and the teasing about wheelchairs and care homes started to feature as much as anything else whenever the topic was discussed, which in truth was not all that often.

However, it is worth considering the grieving process. Many people assume that it refers only to dealing with feelings after a death. This is not the case at all. The grieving process is applicable to any personal loss that causes hurt. This might mean somebody who has a leg amputated grieving for the loss of their leg. It certainly applies to people with Parkinson's who lose function of some sort even when it happens slowly over a lengthy period of time. Awareness of the grieving process can help people to sit comfortably with it or give them a structure within which to talk to friends or relatives about how they feel without being seen as dwelling on bad news or without people thinking they can't mention something in case it upsets you. Certainly life with Parkinson's is peppered with lots of little losses. People who have a healthy, tried and tested structure within which to deal with those losses and to accommodate the new lifestyle that comes afterwards, are more likely to remain on an even keel throughout this ongoing process of change.

This way of understanding loss and thus how to deal with it was developed by a counsellor called Elisabeth Kubler–Ross. Below is an adaptation of what she wrote, and refers particularly to issues to do with death and bereavement. For more detail please see the original work.

All people grieve differently. Some people will wear their emotions on their sleeve and be outwardly emotional. Others will experience their grief more internally, and may not cry. You should try and not judge how a person experiences their grief, as each person will experience it differently.

The first reaction is to deny the reality of the situation. It is a normal reaction to rationalize overwhelming emotions. It is a defence mechanism that buffers the immediate shock. We block out the words and hide from the facts. This is a temporary response that carries us through the first wave of pain.

As the masking effects of denial and isolation begin to wear, reality and its pain re-emerge. We are not ready. The intense emotion is deflected from our vulnerable core, redirected and expressed instead as anger. The anger may be aimed at inanimate objects, complete strangers, friends or family. Anger may be directed at anyone. Rationally, we know that no one person is to be blamed. Emotionally, however, we may resent a person for causing us pain or for leaving us alone. We feel guilty for being angry, and this makes us more angry.

The normal reaction to feelings of helplessness and vulnerability is often a need to regain control—
If only we had sought medical attention sooner...

If only we got a second opinion from another doctor...
If only ...

Two types of depression are associated with managing loss. The first one is a reaction to practical implications relating to the loss. Sadness and regret predominate this type of depression. We worry about the costs. We worry that, in our grief, we have spent less time with others that depend on us. This phase may be eased by simple clarification and reassurance. We may need a bit of helpful cooperation and a few kind words. The second type of depression is more subtle and, in a sense, perhaps more private. It is our quiet preparation to separate and to bid our hopes and plans farewell. Sometimes all we really need is a hug.

Reaching this stage of mourning is a gift not afforded to everyone. A loss may be sudden and unexpected or we may never see beyond our anger or denial. It is not necessarily a mark of bravery to resist the inevitable and to deny ourselves the opportunity to make our peace. This phase is marked by withdrawal and calm. This is not a period of happiness and must be distinguished from depression.

Coping with loss is a ultimately a deeply personal and singular experience — nobody can help you go through it more easily or understand all the emotions that you're going through. But others can be there for you and help comfort you through this process. The best thing you can do is to allow yourself to feel the grief as it comes over you. Resisting it only will prolong the natural process of healing.

Chapter 16 – The Nuclear Option

For several years I had a relatively stable time with my Parkinson's. There was no obvious impact on my abilities. I was taking a relatively low amount of medication for Parkinson's and some for hypertension which may have been contributed to by the Parkinson's and the medication I took for it. (Some of you will know that that's me in denial mode. Whatever the effect of Parkinson's and its medication on my blood pressure the truth of the matter is, I was overweight and relatively sedentary, and I'm sure in reality they were the main reasons for raised blood pressure.) After the initial diagnosis I saw a neurologist a couple of times on an annual basis and then had a break for about three years with no appointments. I later discovered that this was because my local neurologist had retired and the system within greater Manchester hospitals had been reorganised so that all the neurologists were located together at Hope Hospital in Salford and each was allocated to a local district where they ran clinics.

I had changed GP during this time because my own retired rather suddenly and I didn't want to stay at his clinic with one choice of doctor. So I signed up at the large surgery in the centre of town which had a dozen or more GPs and which offered a range of services which normally had to be received at the hospital. I was allocated a named GP and after seeing the nurse for initial tests of height, weight, blood pressure and so forth had an appointment to meet him. He was a very affable man, younger than me but about as large. I thought that was quite a good idea as he was less likely to go on at me about my weight (or so I thought). He was interested in my

Parkinson's and how it was being treated and more importantly how it was affecting me. I had found someone I could talk to who appeared to listen and who had offered his support. I decided I'd made a good move and was happy with the prospect of working with him over the coming years. I really do see the doctor-patient relationship as being one of working together. I cannot stand being done to or not understanding why one thing is more appropriate than another. I believe that this shared approach contributes to a better general state of health and well-being and I also think it's helpful to the doctor when patients take an active interest if they are able.

And so it was after the episode of the vasculitis and a change of my dopamine agonist medicine from one tablet to another that I raised the issue of a neurologist visit with my GP. When I told him how long it had been since I'd seen a neurologist he seemed a bit taken aback and immediately agreed to refer me back to the neurologist at the local hospital.

Eventually the appointment came through. Again the day arrived and again I dressed in my suit still holding desperately onto the belief that what I wore had a bearing on the outcome of the meeting. If that's not true, it is certainly the case that how I dress has a bearing on how I feel about myself in the meeting. I duly arrived at the outpatients, went to the blue section which was still painted blue, reported to the receptionist and once again took a chair for her and carried the sealed envelope with my medical notes round to the relevant waiting area, remembering to be careful to avoid looking at them lest I learned something medical about myself.

The new neurologist was a younger man than me as well. He had a pleasant manner and was chatty and very quickly acknowledged that I had read around Parkinson's disease a great deal. He asked me a lot of questions about progression and did some of the basic stiffness and rigidity tests. We talked about my medication and after a while he said "I'm just wondering whether or not it is Parkinson's at all".

"Funny you should say that" I replied "I have wondered myself a time or two."

"There is a more definitive test now" he said. I raised my eyebrows as I wasn't aware of this. In what was only a few short years ago it was clear that the scans were exclusion tests and the rest of the process was an assessment of symptoms.

"It's called a DAT scan" he went on "what they do is inject a radioactive isotope into your bloodstream. As long as they get the right one any remaining dopamine producing cells are caught up by it and show up on a scan. You can see whether they are balanced on both sides of the brain and how much room they take up. What do you think of trying that"?

"I'm fine trying it" I asserted "as long as it doesn't involve any pain!"

The letter finally arrived with an appointment for some months hence to attend at Manchester Royal Infirmary for the scan. There was quite a bit of information included. It explained that the radioactive isotope was the equivalent to having several x-rays together and that therefore it was advised that people took a course of thyroxin to protect the thyroid before and after having the scan. The prescription for these tablets could be obtained by visiting the GP. The paper went on to explain that on arrival the injection would be given and then attendees are expected to wait for some 3 to 4 hours to allow for the isotope to attach itself to the appropriate cells. The scanning process then would normally last a total of some 40 minutes. Rather worryingly I thought, there was a caution to keep clear of pregnant women and new born children during the time immediately after the injection of the isotope and for some 3 to 4 days. Warnings such as this, whilst entirely appropriate, do also give people pause for thought about what they are doing to themselves in the process of trying to sort out a problem. When I hear someone say for example, that I should have six monthly blood tests to monitor my liver and kidney function I begin to wonder what the drugs I take, which have to be processed by these vital organs, are doing to them as a by-product. I worked on the assumption again that processing the drugs is not a task that these organs were built to fulfil with the frequency and the length of time that they have to for people like me.

So equally, with a nuclear isotope coursing through my veins and rushing through my head, fastening itself willy-nilly to cells it could recognise as dopamine producers "Oi, you, dopey get over here now". The dopamine cell ambles across to the radioactive isotope and is immediately covered in the isotope juice. Looking shocked, it runs back to its home in the nether regions of the brain. That goes on for many hours and I didn't really question openly what damage that might be doing as a consequence of fulfilling its correct function.

When I arrived on the scheduled date at the appointed time at the Royal Infirmary fondly known as the MRI (no, not Magnetic Resonance Imaging.) The waiting area was absolutely packed. I dutifully reported to reception as the signs required and after a little bit of form filling was asked to take a seat. You never know whether the other people sharing a waiting room are there for similar problems or entirely different matters than oneself. As a people watcher I look around and try to put a context on the people waiting with me. Many of them had someone with them. This is not something that we have ever got into. I would tend to go to these appointments on my own. I drive the car and I would usually be going on somewhere or going to the appointment from somewhere other than home. Also many of the people at hospital appointments are retired folk and therefore perhaps it's a better way of spending the time for them. It was clear that there were some people in pain and this again gives rise to the "it could be worse" philosophy. Finally, after about 45 to 50 minutes a nurse came out and loudly mispronounced my name. I waved a hand and ambled over to have the usual discussion about Polish pronunciation. I say this as if it is a wearisome matter. The fact is I love it when people ask about my name. I love explaining it to them. I love hearing them go from the mispronunciation to the correct pronunciation after a short conversation. It can't happen too many times a day for me and it does happen many days of the week. Long may it continue.

I was taken into a side ward given a seat and invited to take my jacket off and roll a sleeve up. The nurse sat down with me, which I thought was a little unusual, then produced a thick set of paperwork. There followed a lengthy explanation of what was happening and what it was that was being injected into me. This was done in simple enough English and it was clearly more of a health and safety activity rather than a medical one. Fair enough, I signed the paperwork and watched as she hefted the syringe from its lead lined container. She explained that the lead jacket around the syringe was for my protection as well as hers and said that she would be as quick as possible in performing the injection. This was duly administered without any problem from my point of view. The syringes were extraordinarily heavy and therefore difficult to manipulate and I should imagine that getting an in-depth injection at the end of somebody's working day would be riskier than at the beginning. I was told that I didn't have to wait in the hospital for the duration which was something of a relief and so I went across to the Whitworth Art Gallery to have a look around and to get some lunch whilst avoiding pregnant women and new born babies. Needless to say, I started to see them everywhere and began to feel a little paranoid about walking past them; my catholic guilt relishing the opportunity to flood my system with little sins. If I were practising, I would have needed to go to confession quickly to clear the way for the nuclear material. Fortunately, as a lapsed Catholic, I recognised that leaving the sins and the guilt within the system serves not only to make me responsible for all the bad things that happen around me but also save time in me trying to get any relief for a very important function. I tried to focus on the nuclear material rushing around my body, heading for the blood brain barrier, breaching it and searching around my brain looking for dopamine producing victims. I felt nothing.

I wandered around the gallery, had my lunch and 2 cups of the refreshing panacea and then went for a stroll along the Oxford Road towards Wilmslow Road and Rusholme. The memories come flooding back every time I'm round there. They are myriad and would take far too long to cover in detail. Suffice to say that this included the street my grammar school was on, the route to the Polish Club in Moss Side and the way to the university – I was never a student there, but spent a fair bit of time socialising. The first thing that always strikes me hard about these memories is that they take me back to that happy time of relative innocence during my childhood and teenage years when the idea of being chronically unwell was completely ridiculous, never mind becoming disabled and all that goes with it. We were young and fit and healthy, relatively well-behaved and trying to establish our adult identities. There, beyond Whitworth Park the Whitworth pub. My first half of mild, at age 13, for one shilling and one penny old money (about 5½ pence in today's currency). Further along on the left is The Clarence, an Irish pub with a bright red door. A regular haunt during one particular period of my life and the place that my workmates from the hospital cleaning team took me on my 18th birthday to get me to drink more than I could or should. What a memory. I recall afterwards cycling home on what appeared to be a six lane highway. I couldn't understand it because I had arrived from a regular two lane main road. Further on, around a corner past St Edwards Church to the gates of Xaverian College. My alma mater; the scene of my secondary education; the institution from which, following my abject failure to pass exams, I launched my adult life. Also the site of many happy memories associated with music and friendships and goings home. Nostalgia. Not a bad thing in small doses.

As a teenager, there's no question that I enjoyed a drink of alcohol as did the majority of my peers. I also got drunk several times. Sometimes excessively so. As did the majority of my peers. It so happened, though, that when I was 18, I was having pains in my stomach sufficiently to take me to the doctors who diagnosed hepatitis 'A' which I understood to be a viral form of hepatitis. The doctor told me to lay off alcohol and fats for six months. That, he believed, should give sufficient time for everything to settle down.

At that age, going to the pub was the usual social activity, particularly midweek. It was difficult to turn up and order a pint of orange juice (nor was it particularly pleasant), but it's what I had to do so I managed to do it. There were plenty of snipes to ward off and lots of puzzled looks as to why I was drinking pints of orange juice, but nevertheless, we survive these things, and the clock never stops ticking. After six months the pains had indeed gone away and I began to drink socially again, in the same pattern more or less as the majority of my peers. Unfortunately, about six months after that, I was struck with pain again and went back to the doctor who suggested trying the same thing for longer. I didn't give a great deal of thought to the implications of this, I just went back to not taking alcohol at all and theoretically at least, reducing the amount of fat I consumed. By this time I had met Dot and our relationship was clearly quite serious. We were at a point when we were able to buy a car. It was cheap and cheerful, but it went and got us from place to place. As Dot didn't drive, that responsibility fell to me entirely. Unlike the majority of my peers. We never had to wonder about who was not going to drink because they were the responsible driver. It was me. And this meant that after the passage of a year not drinking and having reached a time when I could have begun social drinking again, I decided not to bother. I had managed a year without any difficulty, and enjoyed having a car. The idea of inadvertently overdoing alcohol levels and being caught for that was wholly unacceptable and not worth the idea of the odd pint here or there.

At that time, it was decidedly unusual to be teetotal, and people wondered about your motivation and whether or not you actually stuck to what you said you did. Whilst close friends didn't argue, some people got quite shirty if they offered to buy you a drink and you asked for an orange juice. It was as if somehow they felt that I was judging them for drinking, which I wasn't at all. I'm very well aware that in certain parts of Greater Manchester Probation Service over the years there have been people who believe that I was an alcoholic, albeit one who was on the wagon. This is decidedly not the case, but I chose never to discuss this with anybody, nor try to convince them otherwise if they believed that rumour.

One of my party pastimes is watching people and seeing the point at which they just go beyond their safe limit. There is a change; sometimes they become garrulous, occasionally they become very happy, some people become extremely aggressive - and so to be avoided - and some people appear to get very sad. Whilst this fits in with my people watching interests, I've not yet worked out why different individuals have those different reactions, nor indeed if they're consistent. It's probably because we don't go to many parties, so I've not had the chance to ponder it. Anyway, I've always been happy to serve as the driver at social events and I've also always been happy knowing that I've never been at risk of drink-driving.

Back to the scan. It was time to turn about and walk a bit more briskly back up towards the outpatients department of the Royal. I reported in again and took my seat for them and had only to wait about 20 minutes before I was called in.

This scanning machine was even more skeletal than the MRI one. They could clearly pack far more kit into much smaller space these days. There was lots of lead glass around the place for staff to step behind when rays were being fired and I imagined they would keep certain distance from me given my current radioactive state. I lay down this time with practised ease on the platform and was tucked in by two staff with jokey admonishments to 'be still or be in trouble'. They pulled a face guard close over my face. I shut my eyes. Somebody thought to put on some half decent music and I just relaxed. The machine was relatively quiet and moved me around before going click, thump, whirr and then repeating the cycle. It was all over in about 15 minutes and after being helped to sit up and get off the platform (something which does not come with practised ease) I put on my jacket, said my farewells and left. That was now done and I could only await the results coming through. Nobody was going to say when that would happen in any more specific terms than in 'a few weeks'.

Chapter 17- Pardon - I heard that!

After several weeks a letter landed on the mat from the neurologist telling me that the scan showed that I did indeed have idiopathic Parkinson's disease. An appointment was enclosed to see him again in a few months' time and once again, everything went quiet.

At this point I was still relatively stable and on the whole unscathed by Parkinson's and apart from the incidents mentioned suffering relatively little from the medication I was taking. Equally there was no benchmark by which to measure whether that medication was doing anything positively good. It may well have been preventing or slowing down progress of the condition. It may have been making me feel a little unwell all of the time to the extent that that became my norm and I felt well enough that way having forgotten what it felt like not to have such a condition or to take such a cocktail of medication.

Since my diagnosis I had achieved two promotions in my work, first from a senior probation officer to a district manager. The next one was to a post as HM Inspector of Probation. I have never withheld the fact of having Parkinson's. I put this down to having worked in a forward-looking and well structured public service which embraced relatively fully the role of anybody with disability in society. Certainly I never felt that I had been discriminated against because of my condition. There were occasions when I was unhappy however with questions on application forms. I remember applying for an Assistant Chief Probation Officer post in one of the Yorkshire services and having to answer the question on the application form 'would I require assistance to access the office' if shortlisted. I was not shortlisted to that post and when talking to the chief officer to receive feedback as to why I was not selected, I took the opportunity to ask him why he needed to know about access to the office at that stage in the procedure. He, of course explained that it was so that they could ensure that assistance was available particularly for wheelchair users as it was not the easiest of buildings to access. I pointed out to him that he did not need to know that information in order to decide who he would like to interview. It was only after he made that decision that he would need to know whether those candidates coming for interview required assistance. By sequencing the question in this way he would avoid the appearance of perhaps filtering out anybody with a movement disorder at the shortlisting stage. I was gruffly thanked for my comments.

I also happen to suffer from a degree of deafness. I had gone through what I now know to be a typical procedure at home of being told time and again to get my hearing checked as I was clearly going deaf, to which I responded "well if you would speak up I wouldn't have a problem hearing you".

I remember the occasion on which I had no choice but to admit that it was my hearing and not other people's speech that was the problem. Sitting in a large meeting room at headquarters involved in a very worthy, if rather dull, area management meeting. I was sitting at the door end of the room, the quicker to get away at every opportunity. Straight down at the other end, about five or six seats away from me, and sideways on, one of my colleagues was speaking with enthusiasm about a particular topic. He was sitting forward and I was following him perfectly well. Suddenly somebody halfway down the table leaned forward to adjust their papers and blocked the speaker from view. Immediately, his words went from clear to befuddled and then as the middle placed individual sat back, the words became clear again. I felt betrayed by myself and also rather embarrassed at some of the noises I had made on this point. What I realised was that I was, without knowingly doing it, both listening and lip-reading in order to follow what was being said and without both sources together, I was struggling.

I finally succumbed in my early 30s and went for a hearing test. Of course the equipment must have been faulty because it did maintain that I had a hearing loss and the doctor insisted on following what the equipment indicated despite my protestations. I was offered, almost apologetically by the doctor, a national health hearing aid. This is one of the best services I have come across. You are provided with an individually fitted, personally tuned hearing aid. You receive instruction in how to use it and written information to support that. Replacement batteries are free. Re-tubing is free and done for you. All of this service is freely available, provided by people who know what they're talking about, using equipment that on the whole works extremely well. Why on earth would anyone spend hundreds (or thousands) of pounds to have a private hearing aid, many of which I am told don't work very well at all.

On the back of this I have always taken care to consider the arrangements of seats in a room when conducting meetings and interviews. I have been in for job interviews where the interviewing panel has sat with their backs to a window with me facing them. This means that the backlight from the window blocks out their facial detail, making it very difficult for me to follow who's saying what. It can of course be extremely difficult when attending a brand-new organisation and being interviewed by senior staff to tell them how to arrange the room to accommodate a visitor, especially if this means a significant furniture move. However, in smaller settings, people are usually perfectly happy to hear what's being said about interviewing people with hearing difficulties and changes can usually be made simply by people altering their seating positions. My experiences with both Parkinson's and deafness are based at least in part, on the fact that I've spent many years looking after myself appropriately and also the needs of my second son, Richard, who is partially sighted. However I have done nothing at all for other people with disability and as I reach a point in my life where I have some time available I am determined that I will take on and make some provision for, the needs of other disabled people.

Certainly, writing this book, whilst being very therapeutic for me, may well be of assistance to others. That's certainly the view that a number of people have shared with me whether they have or haven't had a look at an earlier version. It would please me very much to produce a book that serves that purpose to some extent. Whilst in no way is this a "guide to living with Parkinson's" type of book, some people may identify some activity, philosophy or approach that may just help them with a particular issue. I know for a fact that that has been the consequence for a number of people who read copies of 'Chapter & Illuminating Verse' the poetry and art book about Parkinsons I co-wrote and published a few years ago.

It has been a surprise to me to hear people speak so positively, not only about enjoying the poems and Ghislaine Howard's pictures, but people have actually said that they found the poetry helpful and this extends beyond people with Parkinson's. People with other conditions, indeed people with far more serious conditions have given unsolicited comments about the way they could relate to the emotions expressed and the way indeed that they found poetry helped them identify feelings that they had not understood. If this happens only for one person then it is, to say the least, gratifying. If it happens more widely then that is such a reward and something in which I take perhaps more pride than I'm entitled.

Chapter 18 – Moving On

The next routine appointment with the neurologist finally came around and I attended the blue suite, reported to the receptionist and took a seat for her. After a while I was summonsed into the consultation room where the neurologist sat with a colleague. After a little of the usual small talk he produced a colour print of the DAT scan. There, before my eyes, was a series of pictures of my brain, the two halves showing reddish/pink areas, one much more than the other. This was the dopamine producing area of the brain and one side was practically gone and the other side he told me was smaller than would be normal. I found this print fascinating and asked how I could obtain a copy. I was delighted when he simply handed it over to me and asked "you will send it back to me won't you".

Having acknowledged the slow progress but now established that it was indeed Parkinson's, he conducted a number of the peculiar little physical examinations that neurologist's seem to be able to tell so much by. He then asked if it was okay if his colleague could do some tests which was of course fine by me. The colleague took hold of my arm and manipulated it, asked me to make various movements and then sat down with a thoughtful look on his face. "There doesn't seem to be an awful lot we can do usefully given the current state of play" said the doctor. "The medication you're on seems to be holding things well enough. I think we have to just monitor things for a while, perhaps annually and react as and when we have something we need to react to. How does that sound to you?" "Well" I replied "it seems a reasonable and logical position. But if I were only seeing you once a year I could have to wait a very long time to report a development to you". "That's no problem" he said you would just contact my secretary and she would put you in on a much shorter appointment if there's something you specifically feel concerned about." At this point I had of course no idea that Parkinson's symptoms were going to start to close in on me relatively soon and I would have a considerably longer list of issues to raise with the neurologist next time I saw him.

It was over a year until I saw him again, in 2008. During that time I continued to work as an inspector of probation, travelling up and down the country leading teams and earning my crust. I enjoyed my work and I enjoyed my home life although work seemed to be getting busier and busier. The boys continued to develop into fine young men. Matt had married and was living and working in Stockport. Richard was just coming to the end of his university course and applying for work in what was undoubtedly a very competitive environment.

Being a parent is one of those jobs you only get one go at with each child. Our boys were quite different from each other in lots of ways but I always considered them to be complementary. They were both changing appropriately, maturing some might say, as they grew older and circumstances changed. The needs that children have from parents vary according to the individual of course and family dynamics and also to the stage of life. We were still the bank almost totally as far as Richard was concerned. Of course if he was to get work that would diminish very quickly as it had done with Matt once he got married and settled with somewhere to live and a job. Financially we are doing well and we were in a position to pay off the remainder of our mortgage without penalty and therefore not needing to have one at all. Quite an exciting prospect from my point of view and one that served to justify the decision I took as a very young man to know for certain that I was going to get paid next month and to accept that the amount would be lower rather than go for boom or bust arrangements where one might make an absolute packet but might also be out of work at the drop of a hat. As I write this I hear the echoes of my father insisting on having life insurance even in his 30s despite mum arguing that she could make better use of the money in the weekly grocery shop. I know this of course only because my mum told me the tale, not from any actual memory. It seems ridiculous that it could be a genetic characteristic and even if it was I don't know how I would identify it as such given that I have no actual memory of my dad. Even if I did have memories of him I am fairly sure that they wouldn't have been about such searching financial matters as the domestic budget. The fact remains that he had such a tendency as do I. But who knows maybe it's just a coincidence?

Along with watching the boys grow and mature, it was noticeable to me that the Parkinson's had certainly progressed. It wasn't a terrible problem but the tremor had become bilateral now. I had one particular day when I was sitting down in London with a pile of papers that needed editing or amending or signing off. As I brought my pen towards the paper that required signature my hands shook so much that I couldn't put the nib to the paper. I tried four or five times, somewhat unbelieving about what I was seeing in front of my own eyes. But the fact of the matter was I couldn't put the pen on the paper. If I had, it would have resulted in an inadvertent scribble all over the document. I was unsure what to do first. This clearly wasn't right but equally it didn't seem like something that the doctor could address. Then I became quite agitated and upset and was cursing Parkinson's in my head. I knew exactly what that was indicative of.. Deterioration. Disability. Dependence. Degeneration.

There was little point in contacting anybody to let them know. I just sat back for an hour or so and had a cup of panacea and then tried again. This time the pen engaged perfectly with the paper and I was able to sign my name. I know that looking at my signature, one might well think I had been having a tremor at the time I wrote it, but that was my normal handwriting. I made a short note of what had happened on that date and carried on my work with scarcely a flutter for quite some time from my unwelcome visitor.

At this point, when I experienced tremor it was certainly of an increased velocity and power. I was from time to time, aware of my medication having worn off and the need to take more. This running out or "wearing off" as it is called manifests itself by slowing me down so that my walk becomes a shuffle and producing a lack of facial expression. It is a very peculiar feeling and hard to describe. It is short of freezing which some of my friends experience, where they literally cannot move themselves for a period of time. I have not yet, at the time I am writing about, had that joy, having always been able to move, albeit sometimes exceedingly slowly. Upon checking, I identified that this was always because I had missed the appointed time for taking the next dose of tablets, due to busy-ness or lack of attention and this had been sufficient time to permit the last dose to be used up. The consequence of this was a speedy reversion to what it might be like without any medication at all. I have many times wondered what it would feel like not to take any of my drugs. Doctors get very agitated when I raise this and warn me of the dire consequences of doing such a thing, even under their oversight. Thus far, cowardice rules.

So it came to the next appointment with the neurologist. I scrubbed up lovely, shone my shoes and set off in good time. At that time, I drove a largish Honda Accord saloon automatic. I tended to park on the road outside the old part of the hospital which was also the location for the local sixth form College. An incredible number of sixth formers have their own cars these days and the roads were jammed solid. I drove around a little expecting a gap somewhere before realising the college would not finish for another two hours. I was loathe to pay the car parking fee charged by the hospital and ultimately reversed into a very tight spot quite some distance from the outpatients department. I got out, threw on my jacket, cleared my bits out of the body of the car and put them in the boot. I set off walking and looked closely at my watch. I felt a bit pressed to realise that I only had 15 minutes before my appointment time. This is the sort of silly anxiety that one can get. I'd never been to one of these appointments and not been kept waiting an absolute minimum of 20 minutes so I couldn't really consider that I was going to be late, but that is how I felt. Anxiety - another side effect of Parkinson's? Many would say so. I don't know. What I do know is I have those experiences far more acutely now than I ever did before diagnosis.

I walked quickly but became a little out of breath. Then I started to sweat. Nobody tells you about the sweating. I'm not talking about the gentle perspiration here, or a ladylike sheen. I am talking about full on, shirt drenching, jacket soaking, sweat. I'm talking about water running from your head down your face and dripping off the end of your nose and chin sufficiently to make puddles on the floor. I'm talking about sweating to dehydration. Nobody ever mentioned it. It took me ages to twig that this was connected with Parkinson's and/or medication.

Picture the scene. It's a pleasant spring day and everybody's happy. You're in Brighton in a reasonable hotel on the seafront. You have a meeting starting at 10 o'clock just about three quarters of a mile walk away. You're meeting the chief officer and chair of the board of the local probation area to discuss the results of the inspection with them. It's an important meeting for them and you're an important person to them. You're wearing a cotton shirt and a Marks and Spencer's lightweight suit, carrying a medium weight bag that has a laptop and various papers in. You also have a small overnight case of decent quality running quietly on good rubber wheels. You set off from the hotel at 9:15 allowing yourself half an hour to get there and 15 minutes for any problems, missing a turning or whatever it might be. You set off at a fair clip, not running but not strolling. You would expect to get warm in these circumstances and so after about a quarter of a mile you slow the pace slightly as the walk is now up a slight incline. The wind is blowing nicely making you feel cool as you go along and at this pace, without any fuss you arrive at the probation headquarters in very good time for the meeting. Into the security area, introduce self to receptionist and was quickly invited in and given the visitors badge and escorted to the meeting room. By this time your cropped hair is a puddle of wet which is now running down the back of your neck into your shirt collar. You escape to the loo to wipe yourself off with paper towels as best you can. The sweating starts up again. You look down and see that your shirt is just a series of damp patches running one into the other. There's not a lot you can do about it. You wipe again with paper towels. It soaks up the mess but the sweat reappears and the clothes already look like an aerial picture of some Eurasian rice fields. This is now twenty minutes after arrival.

You have to go back into the meeting as people are waiting for you. You see the look they give as you enter. There is a little concern expressed; do you want some water, cup of tea etc. What you want is for the ground to open up and swallow you or a time machine take you back to the front door and make you not go in for about 10 minutes. You don't know why you're sweating so profusely but you do know that it's a very embarrassing situation and one that you want to get out of. In another 10 minutes you've stopped sweating and your clothes are beginning to dry. Your jacket will need considerable airing before you feel comfortable to put it on again. This is the first of many, many such mornings and leaves me puzzled, embarrassed, and very uncomfortable.

So it is that I arrive, wet, at the outpatients department (blue section...) reacquaint myself with the receptionist and take a chair for her once again. By the time it is my turn to go into the consulting room I have of course stopped sweating and my clothes have dried, my beard has grown and my nails too.

Well, not quite that perhaps, but a fairly long wait. However it has given me time to order my thoughts and I gave the doctor a reasonably good account of the things that I had noted that had deteriorated. I included the sweating which drew no reaction. This led to a discussion about adding l-dopa medication to my current dopamine agonist. In addition to this I took medication for hypertension and excess acid in my stomach. I had always been resistant to the notion of taking levodopa medication directly because I had read that the earlier it is implemented then of course the sooner in relative terms it becomes dysfunctional. It can also cause difficult side-effects such as dyskinesias which could easily result in losing my driving license, which for me is an absolute lifeline. I explained my reservations to the doctor and he acknowledged them as valid but did go on to say that a low dose of Levodopa was possible with good effect and minimal disruption. We talked about that for a little while and he explained about the potential side-effects of that medication, but went on to say that we seem to be moving now rather quickly to the idea of surgery. This took me aback a little. He had mentioned it in a general sense at an earlier meeting and I had said I was far too scared to undergo that. He now made the point that as the condition was clearly worsening it was likely to continue doing that. I still felt scared; the cost benefit analysis just keeps on changing.

I said that it was something I needed to give thought to. He then suggested what turned out to be one of the best suggestions he had made throughout this strange business. He told me he had a colleague who specialised in Parkinson's who ran clinics at Hope Hospital in Salford (which of course I knew very well) and that his colleague was a movement disorder specialist and would be able to talk to me far more fully and in greater detail about surgery than he himself could. I thanked him for the suggestion and explained that getting to the hospital was no problem at all. He promised then that he would arrange my next appointment to be there and told me that his colleague consultant neurologist was called Jeremy Dick.

Chapter 19 – Give in to Improve

I had heard of Dr Dick. A colleague in the probation service who, coincidentally, had been my practice supervisor when I was a trainee probation officer had developed Parkinson's some years ago and Dr Dick was his consultant. He had been very positive in his comments about the treatment he received. A helpful point of contact was to discover that Dr Dick's wife was a probation officer and had in the past worked in Greater Manchester. I didn't know her but there is merit in belonging to the same organisation I guess. In any event, I am not above clutching at straws if it will give me any sort of edge at all.

Once again, there were several months wait. During these periods of time I'd tended to do my best to forget about having Parkinson's, to forget about the fact of it being a deteriorating condition and simply to get on with whatever it is that I was getting on with. That's usually work and in the recent past has been increasingly work. I find myself doing less and less of the few other activities I enjoy, in part because I'm too tired after work, but also because I find it difficult to come up with enough interest in doing things. I noticed that I was reading less; definitely not me. Still, if I were to get a few decent nights sleep the fatigue might lessen and I might find some space for a few other things.

The appointment letter came in due course inviting me to go to Hope Hospital outpatients to area three. Not as easily identifiable as the blue area, painted blue, at my local hospital I was intrigued to know how I might identify it. A week before the appointment I was inevitably thinking about the topic that was going to dominate the meeting. Surgery. On my brain. A hole in my head. Wires sticking through my brain. Being awake. Being screwed into a head brace. There was a cost benefit analysis to be done here and to me it looked like not doing surgery. I had been a little puzzled that the local neurologist had not said more about dopamine medication which I wasn't yet on. Anyway, it was not to be a meeting where I would consent to anything. I would simply listen to the arguments for or against a surgical approach to managing my admittedly worsening condition.

The day before this appointment I realised that I was really quite worried and so I asked Dot to come with me. This was a first, but I really needed my hand holding and somebody else to hear what was being said. So it was, duly booted and suited, that I drove into my familiar Salford with a new intention. I knew the route to Hope hospital well, as I had been there on a number of occasions whilst a probation officer to visit offenders, following drugs overdoses, violence or failed attempts at suicide. Having parked up in the very crowded car park we walked across to the main outpatient's entrance. There was the usual signage but helpfully two women standing in the corridor who were clearly there to render assistance. I told them which clinic I was looking for and they immediately pointed me down a corridor and invited me to follow the signs to area three. We walked down a wide corridor and turned left. Area three was just part of the wide corridor with about 20 chairs set out. I reported to the receptionist who was just sitting behind a table – no security booths required - and gave my name. She completed the computer database asking me the usual questions: name and address, next of kin, GP, date of birth etc. She then invited us to sit and wait.

After the standard NHS waiting time, which I always allow for now and therefore don't get frustrated about, I was called forward. Dr Dick was waiting to meet us at the door and shook hands and introduced himself. I thought it was a good start and we introduced ourselves and made ourselves as comfortable as one can do on hospital chairs. He looked through the file that he had on me and the referral letter from his colleague and I quickly moved the conversation to mention work and the probation service. He looked up at this point and acknowledged that his partner had worked in Greater Manchester. I then mentioned my friend who was his patient also and as ever with these situations, one felt the atmosphere relax a little and a certain sense of familiarity or comfort slipping in to the setting.

Shortly after this, the conversation turned to business.

"So, you're thinking about surgery for your Parkinson's. Why on earth would you want to take that risk?"

"Well" I said, the relief I was feeling surely obvious in my tone of voice "no, I don't want to take that risk. Your colleague suggested that it was the next or soon to be taken path. I don't want to have surgery at all, especially brain surgery."

"Oh" he commented "well I'm happy to talk to you on that basis. I mean it is an option and although we don't do it here if it's the right thing for you and if you want it I could and would refer you to my colleagues in Bristol for the operation there.

I'm sure though that there is a lot we can do before you need to be thinking about that."

The relief I felt was palpable. The conversation turned to dopamine medication and the pros and cons of it and my concerns about it. All my questions were well answered and I was very impressed with the knowledge that he clearly had about my condition. It was at a much better level than the neurologist I had met at my local hospital. No doubt that was because Dr Dick was a specialist in Parkinson's whereas the others had specialised in different areas. I felt well assessed and that I had had a good explanation of the options open to me. I had agreed to start taking Sinemet (Dopamine replacement medication) and felt that I had a good understanding of what to expect. Dr Dick said he would see me again in three months and then I would be referred back to my local hospital. I held onto that one and decided to tackle it next time.

And so I moved into a new phase of Parkinson's. Taking dopamine medication by mouth, allowing it to run round my system, through my major internal organs where it is not supposed to be, through the blood brain barrier travelling the wrong way and then into my brain where it sets about doing its job from a different starting point than it should. This sounds critical and in some ways it is. On the whole though, I am hugely impressed that this drug has been created and works so well. It literally allows me to move. However, it is some forty years since it was developed and nothing has come near it since then, despite the myriad improvements in pharmacology during that time.

One of the challenges to taking dopamine this way is that, because it shouldn't be in the main internal organs, it can make you feel very nauseous or be sick whilst the body gets used to it. To this end, new users are usually prescribed the drug called Domperidone. This is an anti-sickness drug which combats that side-effect of dopamine very well. It's also the nearest one can get to being prescribed Dom Perignon champagne on the NHS.

As per instructions, I started taking the Domperidone a few days before I started on the dopamine. I had been prescribed Sinamet, which was commonly used for Parkinson's. I was on a very low dose, which was in line with my concerns about starting taking this medication. Much of the research suggests that dopamine is good for about 10 years. Therefore the sooner you start it, the younger you are when it becomes not useful and the younger your life will become a bit more screwed. I had taken this to heart, forgetting of course, that none of us know what is round the corner for us. Why was I sacrificing a better quality of life now for one that may never happen. Equally I could have a better quality of life now being aware that there are significant pieces of research going on which could result in better medication or even a cure by the time dopamine might stop being useful for me. So it was with a less heavy heart than it could have been, that I started these new tablets. The effect was really quite noticeable. By the time I had titrated up to the dosage of three tablets per day which took me about three weeks, I felt generally well. I realised that I had not felt well for a long time. I had come to feel not well slowly, over time and had not realised just what the effect of that had been. Mind you, I could not describe that feeling either, just such an overall feeling of Bleeeeaaagh.

I now felt more energetic and generally lighter. This was a great drug as long as I remembered to take it.

But I also found out that if I missed a dose, it wasn't long before I started to feel quite peculiar. It was as if there was a rotating camshaft in each limb creating an internal tremor at quite high speed which had the effect of pulling the limbs in slightly different directions with just a very gentle bit of pressure. It was not a pleasant feeling and it led to a sensation of being unbalanced. An unpleasant, light drunkenness is perhaps the best way I can describe it. However, I am teetotal, so may have that wrong!

For a while now I had realised that I had from time to time been unsure whether I had remembered to take a dose of whatever medication I was on. I have assiduously resisted using a week-long pillbox, seeing that as yet another sign of giving something up and so giving in to this damned condition. I had used a small silver pillbox just to hold a few tablets initially though it was without compartments and therefore no allocation of doses. However, I started to change when I would feel unwell, wondering whether it was because I needed to take medication but had been unable to establish whether or not I had done so. Being the cautious drug user that I am, I was more scared of taking two doses than of missing one, however unpleasant that might be. Finally I held my hands up and recognised that I needed something to enable me to know with certainty whether or not I take each dose of medication every day. Dot had been telling me this for a long time.

The next time I was in the chemist at the Co-op I decided to see what they had. The most straightforward and cheapest thing seemed actually to be ideal for my needs. Seven plastic strips each of four boxes with click down lids, marked Monday through to Sunday; breakfast, dinner, tea and bedtime on each strip. Four times a day was how often I took my medication and its various combinations and so I could easily fill this each week and be confident of getting my meds consistently.

They were also useful in that each day's worth of boxes could be detached and carried on its own in a pocket which was fine for being at work if I was coming home that evening. Equally all seven sat in a tray which I could put in my suitcase if I was away for the week. It cost £2.50. Money very well spent. Filling the boxes has become a weekly ritual. You have to get all the medication you're going to use out onto the table, take the film covered strips out of the box and pop the pills out of the film covered strip into the plastic boxes. You have to watch that they fall into the right one otherwise you're taking your doses in the wrong order. Happily the colours and shapes help to differentiate when something does fall into the wrong place. If all of the tablets I have were round and white it would be a much harder prospect. I have blue, pink, red, brown, white and yellow in different sizes and very different shapes. (I also have a Blue Diamond one but that isn't taken on regular basis and we don't talk about that too much).

And so I had succumbed. I had given in yet again to Parkinson's. It had dominated me, squashed me and forced out of me a decision I had not wanted to make. I had always recognised that one day I might have to, but that should not be for some time. That being said, I was now able to simply look and see whether or not I had taken any given dose if I became unsure. It was as easy as that. In terms of the time spent filling the weeks' worth of boxes, I figured it couldn't be any more than the time taken to sort out each dose individually which is what I had been doing for the past several years. Altogether I take some 11 different medications across the course of each day, in 21 tablets. There's no point in being terribly inefficient about this. It is a simple fact of my life. I might as well do it the best way possible. I now view the classic pill dispenser boxes with some affection and promote the idea of using one to my friends whenever I get an opportunity. What a turncoat!

Chapter 20 - Slurring, Gasping and Drooling

One of the aspects of my work that I had come to enjoy and at which I considered myself reasonably competent, was giving presentations using PowerPoint. I enjoyed putting the information together on the software and talking to it in front of any size audience. It had taken me some time in my early years as a probation officer to get to that position but having got there and completed some training courses, and delivered training to others it was something I made a reasonable fist of.

Parkinson's affects the movement of muscles. How often I have forgotten that my throat has muscles, my mouth and lips have muscles, my tongue also has muscles and those muscles are as liable to be affected by the vagaries of dopamine levels as the biceps, calves and so on that we think of more immediately.

It was probably about ten years after diagnosis, so in about 2005, that I began to think that I was slurring my speech. I tried to listen for a while and realised that if it was happening, it was happening when I wasn't fully concentrating on pronunciation. I asked one or two people who did not think that it was happening but after several months I became convinced that there was a small degree of slur sometimes in my speech.

When I was diagnosed and told that I had Parkinson's, it wasn't good news of course. But if I'm totally honest, I thought that, when I was a lot older, I would have to deal with shaking and moving slowly and the limitations that would bring. It never entered my head that I might not be able to speak or not move at all or have internal problems. I certainly did not realise that I might be affected in terms of intellect, emotions and so forth. Over the years, as I have educated myself about the condition, I have learned that those things are all possible and I have often taken myself to the land of denial where it is possible to ignore the river of hard truth in which one is standing ankle deep so much of the time.

The idea of having slurred speech was complete anathema to me. Knowing as I do, a number of young onset friends and acquaintances who have been diagnosed for only four or five years and who may still be in their 30s and who have practically unintelligible speech when they are low on medication and are still difficult to follow when topped up, you might be tempted to consider that I ought to recognise the risk of this happening as being reasonably high. It's not as if I am not exposed to the reality of slurred speech by any means. I just don't want it.

You may have gathered that I go to doctors when I absolutely have to rather than when I ought to. I went to my GP once I had come to the view that I was slurring and I asked for a referral to speech therapy. He was in agreement and satisfied, I went home to wait for an appointment. Inevitably there was some time to wait but finally an appointment arrived inviting me to the speech therapy department at the local hospital. I arrived at the hospital and found the unit in good time before my appointment. It was one of the older parts of the building and arrangements were pretty sparse. There were only 3 chairs in the waiting area. Still, only one was required. I didn't have long to wait until a young woman came out of the office area and said hello, introducing herself as Jane. I answered her greeting and introduced myself. She looked surprised when I spoke. I imagine she was more used to people who had overt and significant speech difficulties. She led the away into a small consulting room and invited me to sit. She sat opposite and apologised for the state of the room. She then asked me why I was there.

There was no useful short explanation, so I gave the round the houses story to get to the point where I asked the doctor for a referral. Then I explained a little bit about Parkinson's to her although she seemed to have a reasonable understanding of that. She seemed very doubtful that there was anything to be done and a little perplexed that I was there, even having heard my account and explanation of my concerns. I had spoken about my job and the importance of being able to deliver presentations in a variety of settings and project my voice as appropriate. I decided to acknowledge the relative simplicity of any difficulties I might be having now compared to many of the people that I knew she must work with and this drew a very empathetic response from her. She was quite categorical that it was fine that I was there and that my needs were as important as anyone else's, notwithstanding the extent of any problem that might exist. I found this helpful and comforting as I had started to feel a little fraudulent.

Jane said that she would do some tests with me to see how my mouth and associated body parts were functioning in the construction of sound and volume. This consisted of a number of timed tests with me making repetitive sounds or increasing and decreasing volume, or repeating a pattern of sounds. She timed how many or how much I could achieve in a given amount of time or how long it took for me to achieve four or five repetitions. She then went through the scoring with me. On the first set of tests I had scored above average in all, which was quite a relief to know but also puzzled me as I still felt that I had been slurring slightly. The second set of tests however showed lower scores, some in the average column but a number just seemed to be below average, and this helped to explain the issue. My tongue was not working at the same speed as the rest of my mouth and this could occasionally start to sound like a slur. Fortunately for me, Jane had a set of exercises that could be done to help tackle this. In some respects this might appear to be a rather minor issue. Some of the time I slightly slurred some of my words. Not the worst thing in the world and certainly not something routinely to bother a busy health professional with. She had people who have had strokes, major surgery or serious accidents and who are in desperate need of being given the basics of communication to work with, rather than tidying up the subtleties.

That being said the impact of appearing to slur my words in a number of the situations in which I would often find myself, would reflect not only on me but also on the Probation Inspectorate. It would be bad enough reflecting on me, given my role and the way I like to present myself. How much worse though, to have my colleagues being the butt, perhaps of whispers, perhaps of out and out, in your face comments about inspectors having 'too much to handle' at lunchtime or 'liquid lunch brigade' thrown at them. We have all worked very hard over the past years to change the reputation of the Inspectorate to one that is serious but fair, thorough and challenging but reasonable. It can take a long time and a lot of effort by a lot of people to make a reputation better and very little by one person to make it an awful lot worse.

Anyway, Jane spent 10 minutes with me looking at some diagrams and a model of the structure of the neck and throat and mouth. She then began sticking lollipop sticks in my mouth in various places with instructions to hold them for as long as possible between my lips or with my teeth. There were also a series of sound production exercises that she thought would help. She told me I needed to do these every day and come back in three months' time when she would retest and see how I got on. This seemed to be entirely reasonable, as many of them were exercises I could do in the car I could make as much noise as I wanted. Best of all, she confirmed my query about the value of singing out loud. She said she had no doubt at all that it was beneficial not only for the voice but also for the spirit.

This was bittersweet. I had always been a singer and had stopped when Conrad died. Not in a conscious sense. I just didn't want to anymore. Although I'm mainly talking about singing to myself as I wandered around doing those routine tasks that we all do. I also sang with purpose. In school, as well as playing in the orchestra and the brass band, having lessons on the piano and French horn and then subsequently, the trombone, I was also a member of the choir and prior to that the operatic society. My operatic highlight was as one of the chorus of geisha women in Gilbert and Sullivan's Mikado. I was so made up my mother could not pick me out of the crowd on stage. Aged 11 at the time, 1966 the first year of grammar school, I learnt that the dramatic part of theatre was not for me. What I enjoyed was singing and playing music. Dramatic interpretation or even crowd movement was not for me.

When I was 14 or so I got my first guitar and together with some good friends we formed a band. Although we mainly enjoyed rehearsals we did get booked for 2 or 3 decent gigs which went down well as I recall. I was the singer in the band and would also play rhythm or bass guitar as required. I continued to sing and play guitar into my early 20s, sometimes alone, sometimes with others: but I always sang to myself. I had to recognise that starting to sing again didn't mean that I was forgetting about Conrad. It might mean however, that I was learning to manage that part of my life a bit better.

One of the odd consequences of beginning to sing again was that I noticed I was running out of breath before the end of the line. I then realised, one day whilst delivering a presentation to the team at work that this had begun to happen when I was talking. On my next visit to Jane at speech therapy, I raised this with her. She listened to it happening and fortunately was able once again to provide me with a series of exercises and approaches which she said would help me manage my breathing better. This certainly worked and for a while the problem disappeared. Recently however, I have noticed it return. Unfortunately I can't remember the exercises and need a refresher and will have to make an arrangement for another session of speech therapy. This time around it is not only affecting my speech but I have recently taken up saxophone lessons (about which, more later) and it is affecting my ability to play long notes. Fortunately there are exercises to do on the saxophone to practice extending one's breathing and I'm hopeful that this may be a sort of self-help that would once again do the trick, at least for a little while.

Another, far less lovely aspect of Parkinson's which one reads about but cannot imagine happening, is drooling. Yes, the leaking of saliva from the corner of her mouth running down the chin and dropping off onto one's shirt or other surface. Or, far worse, standing next to somebody looking down at a piece of work on a desk and opening one's mouth to speak, only to find drops of saliva falling onto the page in full sight of both oneself and whoever else happens to be looking. This is shocking when it first happens and both funny and alarmingly embarrassing most of the time.

This has become worse and so on my most recent visit to Jane I raised this and asked her about it. She explained that with Parkinson's, it is very common to swallow less frequently than would be usual. This results in a build-up of saliva in the mouth greater than would ordinarily be there and that pool rises higher in the mouth than would otherwise be the case. Once this body of liquid reaches the lips it is a small matter for it to find a route out and dribble down the chin. It was with a heavy heart that I heard Jane further explain that it was actually a very difficult symptom to manage. Preventing the saliva building up would require additional medication which would in fact impact on the production of saliva and thereby cause other problems by there not being enough of this important liquid to do the job it does for us day in day out without us really being aware of it. Being conscious of the issue is about the best treatment available, and consciously swallowing whenever one becomes aware of a build-up or simply remembering to do so. I regularly find my beard wet and wipe it dry feeling annoyed, embarrassed and amused at the same time.

This impact on the swallowing reflex is similarly found with blinking. Parkinson's causes people to do those activities less often. As a result the eyes get drier than they should, because of the longer gap between blinks in the same way that the mouth gets filled with saliva as mentioned above more than it ordinarily would. If one can remember to blink or swallow more often, then these occurrences would be alleviated or avoided. What is fascinating though is the difficulty that I certainly found trying to remember to do those particular activities when involved in just about anything else. It was the same with walking. The physiotherapists were encouraging me to walk more slowly and in a more organised manner than I had been and whilst I could see the value in what they were suggesting, I could only manage when I concentrated on the actual business of walking. As soon as I would think of anything else such as where I was walking to, what an interesting person just passed by, or look at the building, gosh I have to cross the road now, then my walking would revert to its established bad habit until I realised that and once again, corrected my gait deliberately. All of these activities are automatic and that is why we don't think about them. I'm absolutely sure that this would be almost impossible for anybody who didn't think, as they would have to focus on three activities to keep them all going. Anyone who was a broad thinker is really going to struggle to use focused thinking to manage voluntary movements. So it becomes a question of compromise yet again. The art of the best I can do. Do what you can to manage it as best as you can and the rest you learn to live with. Lots of little losses.

Chapter 21 - Research needs people

I am reasonably committed to the concept that if you have a problem you should try to contribute to its solution. This is not easy, as much of the work around Parkinson's is highly complex technical work. However there is scope for active involvement by people with Parkinson's in taking part in some of the research that is going on. So far, I've been a volunteer on three specific pieces of research and am acting as a commentator on the development of the third.

I find it all fascinating. The first piece of research I was involved in was working in broad terms on cognitive issues. It was a feature of the research that participants were not told what was being looked at or for, as there was a concern that this would then have a bearing on people's responses. It involved me in travelling over to the Manchester Royal infirmary Hospital on four occasions. There was a lot of activity, responding to various shapes and colours presented on a computer monitor, a series of what appeared to be dexterity tests and some straightforward memory questions involving sequences of number etc.

The second project was to do with the effect of Parkinsons on what are known as the 'back-office" skills. Admin, planning, speed, organisation, memory etc. The aim was to see what the impact of practice might be. Initially, two researchers came to our home to explain everything in detail and then I undertook a number of exercises and completed various questionnaires to form a benchmark against which to check progress. A week or two later the program began which involved a researcher coming to our home each day (apart from Sunday) for a fortnight. They supervised me practicing various activities and completing a range of questionnaires and so forth. They also came three months later to run through the tests again.

These were perfectly easy research programmes to agree to take part in as it was entirely non-invasive and involved no pain or discomfort whatsoever. Surprisingly to me, the researchers found it difficult to get enough volunteers for each programme.

The third piece of research was looking into the effect of dopamine medication on swallowing. This of course moves onto an area which can be extremely serious and even fatal. People with Parkinson's often suffer difficulties with swallowing and gagging can be a consequence of that often resulting in hospitalisation at least. I thought it well worth contributing to the possibility of some direct benefit in future years. This was slightly more uncomfortable albeit more entertaining. The research was being conducted at Salford hospital where I go for my regular checks with Dr Dick. The idea was that there would be a series of recorded tests carried out after I hadn't taken two doses of dopamine medication. I would then take my next dose of medication and once it had kicked in the same tests would be repeated. Clearly this would be one way of assessing impact.

There were three broad areas being tested. Breathing tests and lung capacity, reactions between specific areas of the brain and the swallowing muscles measured by discharging electromagnetic pulses over a specific area of the brain and measuring the response. The third set of tests involved sitting in front of an x-ray video whilst swallowing a series of spoonsful of barium, each of different consistency.

The breathing tests were straightforward and simply involved blowing through different tubes in different ways. The x-ray video simply involved sitting me next to a special camera with boards pressing as close as possible up against the platform that was part of the machine. This was not comfortable as such but it was not in any way problematic. Swallowing barium is an easy matter, it is just not the most pleasant material especially when one has not been able to eat or drink for over 12 hours. The link between brain and swallowing is a complex one. There was a narrow tube of electronics that had to literally sit halfway down my throat which meant I had to swallow it and then it had to be held in place. This of course kicks off the gagging reflex. It took me a few goes to get it down initially but once in place I was able to retain it for the duration of the tests and whilst it was not at all problematic it was a little uncomfortable. What surprised me most of all was that the discharge of the electromagnetic pulses above my head were rather like somebody tapping me on the head with a teaspoon. I found this quite surprising as they were over 100 discharges in each set of tests, all on different points of the skull, I did at times wonder whether there was the risk of any damage, although I had been assured that there was not. Had there not been the clicking sensation it would not have occurred to me to wonder about it. However once again it could not be said that this was painful or problematic, merely a little uncomfortable. When weighed against the potential benefits of the learning that would come from this project it was very well worthwhile.

This type of research by design needs to deal with members of the cohort being researched on an individual basis. Each one is a half day working with the person involved followed by all of the analysis and assessment and reviewing of other forms of record, and given that there are probably as many as 40 individuals to be worked with because a cohort of less than 20 couldn't be considered to be giving reliable data, then it is no wonder that it takes several years to complete a PhD or postdoctoral level project.

My second involvement with the swallowing research didn't take place until 2015. It was the same researcher still based at Salford hospital. I was pleased to be contacted as it helps me to feel that I'm making a contribution to others. This time I was again required not to take dopamine beforehand, but on this occasion it was for a much longer period of time. Certainly I was not able to drive in, travelling instead by train and taxi. All the expenses of this are covered by the project so that nobody is out-of-pocket by becoming involved. As well as the paper-based assessments, there was again the opportunity to watch a video x-ray of my skeleton swallowing barium. The kit was upgraded from last time and seemed to work rather better. Highlight of the day though was the hour and a quarter in the MRI scanner. How do I describe this? My task, not on the face of it too challenging, was to lie down for an hour and a quarter. Those of you who have been inside an MRI scanner will know of the variety of sounds that it makes and the incredible volume that most of them are at.

I'm quite deaf and wear two hearing aids. The first time I approached the scanning area they both started to switch on and off, affected by the powerful magnetic field. The hearing aids come out which normally leaves me struggling to hear very much and a pair of ear defenders were put on my head. Even so, it was the volume more than the oddness of the sounds from the machine for the hour and a quarter it ran which stood out. It was certainly loud enough to stop me falling asleep. The bed on the machine is perfectly comfortable, the temperature of the room is pleasantly warm and there is a stream of fresh air being blown up onto your face so that there is no sense of any breathing difficulty. What else would you do but fall asleep. Oh yes the light level is quite low. All I had to do for the hour and a quarter apart from lying there was to hold the "get me out of here" button without pressing it unintentionally and on indicated occasions as in when a particular coloured circle appeared on the screen. At this point I had to perform a dry swallow action which was no doubt causing all manner of lights to flash on the recording of the MRI.

There was another interesting experience during this session of research. Having had many hours with no dopamine I was very aware of being slow and stiff of movement, more so than I normally get - although it is hard to measure these things precisely. Anyway it was certainly a significant degree of major symptoms. Towards the end of everything I took my appropriate dose of tablets. I was sitting in an armchair talking to the two researchers who were completing one or two of the paper assessments by a Q&A method. Twenty five minutes after I'd taken my tablets I felt as if somebody had switched off a constraint device of some sort. I could feel my whole body relax and normalise. This was much more dramatic (not Shakespearean but still good local amateur) than I had previously experienced and again told me a great deal about what Parkinson's was doing to me.

My final thought on this topic is to comment on the attitude of the researchers. On every occasion that I have been to any of these events, I have been made extremely welcome. Every consideration that could be made in terms of access to toilets, help getting up and down from chairs et cetera, refreshments if it's possible, and one's general comfort has been at the front of the researcher's engagement. There have been no distant dismissive attitudes that I've come across. On the contrary I have been made to feel important and that has gone a long way to solving any issues of discomfort that might crop up. Whilst I would probably draw the line at being a guinea pig for drugs, the sort of research that I've described above would always attract me, so that if I was able to contribute to it I think it would be likely that I would put myself forward.

Chapter 22 – Move it

Physiotherapy is a treatment that seems to be viewed variably within the wider Parkinson's community. I think I would have considered myself to be a little sceptical, not about whether physiotherapy could have benefits for an individual or a specific function but that it could do general good for people with Parkinson's.

It's about 5 years after diagnosis. My right hip hurt. Every step I took caused a pain to jag through the joint. Going up and down stairs, I was hesitant because of the pain in the knee as well as the hip. It felt as if it was locked slightly out of place and however I tried to snap it back into place it won't go. It was beginning to affect my life in a wider sense and I was not happy about it. At the time, I have to say, I did not associate it with Parkinson's at all. And then my back began to hurt. It wasn't the hurt you get from gardening or pulling a muscle doing some physical activity. It wasn't the hurt you get from something being stuck in you. It was just a general hurt that radiated and it was wearing.

A number of people had urged me to try physiotherapy, but with it being a medical intervention I was not wildly enthusiastic at the prospect of that being the resolution to these difficulties. Nevertheless after a little more 'suffering' I relented and went back to my GP and explained what I was experiencing to him. He made a connection with Parkinson's, which I still had not twigged (duh). He said that he would refer me to the local physio department at Shire Hill Hospital on the edge of town and that he wasn't keen to prescribe painkillers, that I should try and get by with a few paracetamol or ibuprofen until the appointment. I hadn't expected much else in truth so didn't raise any issues with him, just thanked him for his time and went home.

An appointment came through rather more quickly than I had expected and I presented myself at the reception window at the appointed time. I'm sure I'm not an easy patient, and I'm certainly not a patient one. I didn't know what to expect but I wasn't interested in simply being told what movements to make or being stuck in a group with a bunch of other people who had Parkinson's and told to throw the ball around. I was ready to find problems with staff attitude and lack of ability with people and to leave. I could not have been more wrong.

The woman who came to call me and was small and smiley. She was very welcoming and was concerned immediately for my well-being. She was attentive and considerate but professional. We spoke for some time about what had brought me to this point and she asked me to walk around and do various other movements while she watched and she then set about explaining to me exactly what happened to my skeleton and musculature to cause me to be as I was. Her explanation made complete sense and she then explained what she proposed to do to correct it, which again made complete sense. She raised the issue with me of joining a group of others with Parkinson's but did not apply any pressure about this. I explained my reasons for not wanting to. In large part this is to do with the nature of my job. It is impossible to commit to a regular event such as a night class or a hobby group, simply because one never knows precisely when one will be available on any given evening. Certainly what we do know is that we are away a considerable number of weeks in the year for all or part of the week and regular commitments go by the wayside. That being said I would be reluctant in any event as I'm not a group person. I guess that begs a little analysis but I'm not going to do that here. She fully accepted my position and the matter was closed.

What was even more heartening was that as well as addressing the presenting problem she recognised the underlying problems caused by Parkinson's and offered to see me on a weekly basis for some time to help me to address that as well, once the hip problem had been sorted out. She explained that she was neurological specialist physio and so was not limited to a few sessions on my hip.

Over the course of the coming year I went through three sets of appointments with her by the end of which I was walking straight and had no pain in my hip. I understood what had happened and I recognised the part Parkinson's was playing in it and I had had a good time getting there.

At this point Liz the physiotherapist concerned, was about to move on to pastures new and it seemed a reasonable time for me to stop attending physiotherapy sessions. I knew the exercises I had to do and I did not want to try and engage with a new therapist immediately after such a positive experience with Liz.

One of the difficult things to accept about Parkinson's is that it is permanent and degenerative. Even though certain things can be improved through medication or physiotherapy or by another approach, at the end of the day it is a condition that will get worse and will disable you to a greater or lesser extent. This, for me, has an effect on my motivation to tackle its consequences. I had learned a series of exercises to do which would be helpful generally. I understood why they would be helpful and how they would work. I understood that they would bring about improvement and may also defer some deterioration, but I also knew (and this was the dominant feeling), that Parkinson's would win. It was not going to go away and in the absence of a cure, the best one could hope for was that it was going to be mollified by degrees. It would still come back and get me one way or the other. This is a disheartening reality. For me it also meant that when faced with choosing between half an hour doing exercise or reading my book I would choose my book because what was the point of doing half hour exercise when the bastard was going to grind me down anyway. This way to depression.

To my embarrassment, this has recently happened again. When I went off sick at the end of July 2010 I referred myself back to the SPRINT team who carried out an assessment. This identified, with my agreement, a referral to the physiotherapist, the psychologist and later on, speech therapist. The physio assessment was because I reported some difficulty with my walking. The service I received was again excellent. My walking was assessed, the problems identified were explained to me and the solution was explained, demonstrated, practised and supported. I've moved as a result of this intervention from going up on the balls of my feet and tottering forward, a very risky way of walking in terms of the likelihood of a fall, to setting out walking heel-toe and more slowly. I've also been given a series of exercises to strengthen my core muscles which are based on Pilates. After my initial enthusiasm for the exercises and for practising walking as well as trying to do a little more day-to-day walking activity, things initially went very well and I had a quick improvement. Since then however I have slipped for the same reasons described above. There is one difference now and that is the fact that I am retired. I felt the benefit of the learning and I'm pleased at the changes I have made. The only barrier now is attitudinal or perhaps psychological and therefore something that I can undoubtedly deal with. As I write this on the last day of 2011, and one of the most eventful years in my life, I am giving serious consideration to the whole question of exercise and improvement or at least maintenance of as much function as I can.

Chapter 23 - Pull Yourself Together

One of life's difficult to answer questions is "what is the difference between being fed up and being depressed?" What is the issue of degree here? Where is the line to be drawn? Who draws the line and how do you know if people are faking it?

As a younger man I was not the most patient person around these issues. Yes being fed up was fine, but calling it depression and being ill was taking it a step too far. Then, as I started to think more about things I decided that there was probably a personality type that had a tendency toward mental health problems at the level of depression and other personalities that most certainly did not. I was of course in the latter category. I was a fixer, a healer, a leader, a sorter-outer and I was not inclined to consider myself liable to suffer from depression.

Pride comes before a fall. I have little pride left.

I more or less coped with the death of my son. There was a process to be gone through which I understood and could think about and identify my feelings and behaviours against. Now that was an event that could have made anyone crumble and could have resulted in depression if anything could. It didn't get me then. Or at least, not as far as I was aware.

Unsurprisingly, people have worked on identifying symptoms that are indicative of depression as long as a sufficient number of them are present or they have been in place for sufficient length of time. A person who is depressed will typically have one or both of the following key symptoms almost continuously for a number of weeks:

low mood

lack of interest in or pleasure from usual activities and interests

Still, even with the above applying, are you really depressed or is it a lack of application? So further sub-symptoms have been identified, allowing assessment of depression to be more finely detailed and based upon more and often better evidence. The person may therefore also have one or more other symptoms, including:

difficulty in concentrating
poor energy
appetite disturbance, usually connected with
weight loss, but sometimes also
increased appetite and weight gain
tiredness
difficulty in sleeping – (waking in the early hours of the morning can be a classic sign)
decreased libido (lack of sexual energy)
feelings of worthlessness or hopelessness,
guilt or shame
slowness of thinking
in severe cases, suicidal ideas and thoughts of self-harm

So now there is a much better approach to identifying whether somebody is in fact depressed or simply fed up. Of course it requires the medic to not only know this information but also to elicit it from the patient without leading them into answering one way or another and without giving clues as to symptoms they might want to flag up in order to identify themselves as depressed.

I have been diagnosed as depressed probably four times so far. Each has been different in its manifestation, albeit with similarities evident. I have been treated each time by antidepressant medication and some time off, which has had the desired effect.

My experience with doctors has varied enormously and has ranged from very good assessment, using a structured questionnaire, through to somebody spending most of the consultation trying to find an antidepressant that I could be prescribed that did not clash with my Parkinson's medication.

It is relatively easy to walk into a doctor's consulting room and describe a short set of symptoms that would lead to a diagnosis of depression. Obviously there is no objective test. The doctor's responsibility is to make their best assessment on the information available which includes that provided by the patient. If the patient lies it is very difficult for the doctor to be held responsible for an incorrect diagnosis. However the process of eliciting information from the patient is their responsibility and is not simple. It involves asking basic questions such as "have you thought about hurting yourself or killing yourself"? Further questions such as have you stopped watching TV or stopped doing hobbies or other activities you have normally enjoyed are also useful. It can of course be very difficult talking about a chap's sex life and asking if they can manage to maintain an erection may not be the best footing on which to navigate what may well be a very sensitive and delicate relationship. I realise as I look back on what I have just written that it may say more about myself than it does about anybody else. Well, I'll leave that to the reader to determine. However – back to the business of assessment for depression - it is possible after asking specifics to close with a very open question such as "is there anything else going on in your life that you think may have contributed to how you feel"? This achieves two important ends. The first is as an open question that, framed this way opens the door to the individual to tell the doctor anything at all that they haven't already mentioned. The second is that it reasonably puts the responsibility squarely on the shoulders of the person concerned to do this. These are both entirely reasonable outcomes as far as the Doctor is concerned and indeed if honestly responded to also best for the person concerned.

Depression is a common illness. I think the latest figures show that something like 10% of the population suffer from depression at some point in their lives. This is a big issue with major implications for the economy and for family life. It is a difficult issue for doctors but they take on their role in the knowledge that they could have difficulties and I don't believe there is any excuse for not taking the assessment of mood seriously.

I mentioned before that I have had four episodes of depression. The first episode occurred when I was working as a project leader in the Home Office at the time. It was probably about 1997 and had been diagnosed two years and on medication for that time. My manager at the time did not know how to do the job that he was being paid for. His manager was all over the place. The supplier of the IT equipment etc was running rings round the civil servants in terms of pricing and activity as well as equipment spec. I was being told to go out and 'sell' what I considered to be a fairly pathetic, underspecified and unpleasant system and set of equipment to probation areas, many of whom had no desire whatsoever to touch this with a barge pole. I was not a happy man and my arguments had fallen on deaf ears at every turn. Yes, I did have some victories and managed to bring some improvements into the specification, but these were small and did not remove the overriding reality that the government was going to expect the probation service to use this and save money on the back of it. I knew and my grade colleagues on the team knew that this was an impossibility and if anything it would generate costs rather than save them. This clash of beliefs put me in a position I had never before been in. I did not know how to deal with it.

I would go to bed at night feeling anxious and tense. I was unable to sleep and this would make my anxiety worse. I was aware of my heart pounding, my breathing being shallow and of profuse sweating. By the time I went to the GP I was a physical and emotional wreck. No sooner had I started to tell him how I was feeling than I was in tears in front of him, which added to my embarrassment no end. He talked to me for a while, explaining that feeling stressed caused adrenaline to be permanently pumped into my bloodstream. It is designed to be a short-term fight or flight chemical which is produced when needed and used for a short dramatic burst of energy. When it is continually produced it poisons the system. Result: depression (exacerbated it is fair to say by both my condition and other medications that I was taking). He prescribed an old-fashioned tricyclic antidepressant, because of the Parkinson's medication that I was on which could clash with an SSRI, the more modern drug of choice for mild depression. He told me to take time off work and do things that I enjoyed. Imagine somebody telling you to do that, giving you permission not to be at work and to be doing pleasant things like walking in the park or playing with your children. It was like a breath of wind and sun together inviting me to get better. I did take the time off work, which was when I discovered that that was where the pressure was mainly coming from.

As mentioned, these are my own reflections and thoughts based on experience, discussion and reading. It seems to me right to consider depression as being caused by a chemical imbalance in the brain. The challenging question is what causes the disparity to occur in the first place. The last paragraph describes adrenaline production being permanently on as one possible explanation for an imbalance. I also mentioned my Parkinson's as a possible factor. I do not know whether this is reasonable or not and I'm not pointing fingers at any member of any of the professions involved in this area of work. It seems to me that first of all, we know that the substantia nigra (the part of the brain that produces dopamine) has stopped working, albeit not necessarily why. We know that there is a lack of dopamine, whatever method of replacement or support is in place. Therefore, it is reasonable to say that the brain is not functioning as it should. It is equally valid I believe, to consider that any medication taken for Parkinson's will have an effect on brain chemistry. Most of the drugs have been tested for side effects, including serious ones that would also include depression. What I'm not aware has been tested are the combinations of these medications and what issues that might present. It may well be valid to extrapolate from the individual drug tests to a collective set, but I would prefer it thoroughly tested in the combinations that are normally used. This would give us some pegs in the ground with which to be thinking about addressing the problems caused by this challenging aspect of health.

Chapter 24 – and again

The second occasion of depression was I think, more straightforward and more related to my Parkinson's and my medication. My friend Richard died. I'm talking about the Richard who first caused me to go and see my doctor. A good, true friend for 25 years who died suddenly aged 59. A friend who I would talk to several times a week by phone and with whom I would meet up once and often twice a week for coffee and a chat. With our wives we were a happy foursome and did get together for dinners and occasionally went out together. I had been driving home on Tuesday evening and had phoned him to ask after his health and to arrange our next little get together. He had been retired on ill-health grounds because of the impact of two silent heart attacks that he apparently had experienced over recent years and he was not in good health generally. We chatted for a while exchanging jokes and silly talk as well as catching up with each other's news. I arranged to see him next day. At about three o'clock the next day Dot, my wife, phoned me at work which was a pretty unusual event and told me that she had heard that he had died late the previous night. I was confused and bothered as I had not heard anything. I quickly lost concentration on my work and headed home intending to call in at Richard's house en route. I did so and had the terrible news confirmed.

I did what I could during the following week or so to help with arrangements, although it is right to say that Sheila, Richard's wife, was exceptionally well supported by both hers and Richard's family. I was humbled to be asked to speak at the funeral service and of course agreed that I would. I had been the best man at Richard and Sheila's wedding, so in an unhappy sense, this was coming full circle.

So there was a significant event. Indeed a life changing event for many people, including me. I lost a friend, somebody I saw regularly, somebody in whom I confided, somebody who could not be replaced. And without a doubt, I miss him. After a few weeks, I began to feel at a bit of a loss as he was the friend I saw probably the most frequently, albeit often for only short periods. And he was no longer there. But he had not prepared me for his leaving and I felt angry and deserted and sad for him and for me.

This time it was not stress and anxiety that took me along to the doctors. It was a protracted level of low mood and lack of interest in too many things. This time, I was able to take an SSRI because of the medication changes over the years. I only took a short time off work as truth to tell I felt better rather quickly. That is a relative comment of course. I felt well enough to work, not that I felt well per se.

This raises one of the key differences between grieving over bereavement and grieving over a progressive, deteriorating condition. In a brief moment there is a hard fact to be faced. A person has gone from one's life and an adjustment has to be made. That can be a large or small change for different people. They can take a long or short time and need more or less or no help at all. With a condition like Parkinson's there is this steady state of loss after loss after loss. Each one needing to be adjusted to as a hard reality. Each one being a large or small change for different people that can take a long or a short time and need more or less or no help at all. No sooner has an individual adjusted to the change, for example in walking than they experience perhaps a new change of drugs which requires them to make lifestyle changes and so forth. So the frequency and continuity of loss requires each person to be continually going through a grieving process which can be in itself an exceedingly difficult thing to do. There seems to be little recognition of the losses caused by Parkinson's requiring the individual to grieve. There is little or no help available based around the grieving process that I'm aware of and certainly I am absolutely clear that my knowledge of that process and the stages of grief and the iterative nature of the grieving process have all helped me to cope better than I might otherwise have done.

The third time I experienced depression in 2010, the story is really quite straightforward. In a nutshell I consider that I ran out of steam. Slowly over months it took me longer and longer to do more or less anything and in order to continue to achieve at my work I began to stop doing things for myself because it was taking me longer to get things done for work. Thus, reaching the point where looking back I can see that I stopped doing pretty much everything that was not to do with work. I was not reading, something I have done on a daily basis all my adult life. I was not listening to music. I was not even watching TV. I was working and watching the Parkinson's forums on the Internet. I coped for some time this way but again looking back recognise that I was feeling empty. I led a large inspection of a probation area which was complex and far from home and was then due to conduct some very important focused inspections on a particular area's work with dangerous offenders. This had been my meat and drink for several years but the closer the start came the more anxious I realised I was becoming.

It's hard to describe why I call it anxious. There was nothing that I needed to do that I haven't done many times before. The topic was one around which I had extensive knowledge and experience and I had worked in the area on a number of occasions in the past. The colleagues I had to support me were a first rate team. Nonetheless I had a feeling of despondency and gloom about what should have been a perfectly enjoyable piece of work.

I had looked at the work schedule ahead and identified an inspection that I really did not want to lead, although again I'm at a loss as to be able to explain why. Nevertheless I had a chat with my boss and explained that I was feeling overloaded and after some discussion that inspection was taken off me and I was put as a support inspector on one nearer to home. That certainly felt better and for a few days I thought I would manage, but then the dread came. This is a very difficult thing to describe and not particularly easy to admit to. I sat late one night realising that I was actually fearful of the work I had in front of me. There were very few days before it was due to start and I knew that standing down would put somebody else in a pressure situation. I didn't want to do that either to my colleague or to my bosses and I kept arguing with myself in my head that I must go and finish this piece of work at the very least. The hard, harsh reality that bit me was that I actually couldn't do it. Not because of lack of knowledge or skill but simply because of anxiety. It was the realisation of this late at night that made me determined to speak to the doctor and see what he said. I felt very low and was weepy – not a set of feelings I enjoy having and certainly not anything I would want to indulge in. I made an appointment next day but unfortunately was only able to see a locum. His assessment was weak in that he didn't have any structured questions for me he simply asked me what the matter was and I told him how I felt. He asked if I minded going back on medication and I said to him that I simply needed to get better and would do what it took. He then tried to prescribe me an appropriate tablet but kept finding conflicts with my existing cocktail. After he had looked up about 20 different antidepressants he found one which was not going to react with the rest of my tablets. When I asked him about work he said it was up to me but that he would be quite happy to give me a note for a fortnight if I wanted one. This wasn't what I had expected, but I asked for the note in any event figuring that if he thought objectively that I was actually fit he would not be prepared to support me staying off.

The following day I recognised that I had to stop. I had been prescribed antidepressants based on my account of how I felt which had been honest and as detailed as I could make it. I think depression is a nebulous concept and given the lack of an absolute medical definition to use, many people including myself, have great difficulty in accepting it as a label. Nevertheless, it was a vehicle by which I could stop the pressure that was making me feel so bad about something that I enjoyed so much. I had, on several occasions, arrived home and after shutting the front door, simply broken down.

Having got to this point I telephoned my boss Liz, and told her the position I was in. She was as ever, hugely reassuring and supportive and managed to leave me not feeling as bad as I thought I ought to feel. She reassured me that all outstanding bits of work would be taken care of and that people would do that willingly and not be at all resentful, rather wishing that I would get well. I found this difficult to accept and my sense of being a fraud was heightened. Surely I could manage to do what I was paid to do. Surely I could go and inspect a piece of work and stay awake. Surely I could finish my notes at a reasonable hour of the evening and not be sitting until midnight and beyond trying to get them into some sort of shape. No, dammit! No! I couldn't do it. I was burnt out or exhausted or some-such description. If I went to work and failed, then in many ways that might be worse than what I had done, which was to stop with a number of people around me telling me that that was the sensible move. It didn't feel like it, but I set off on two paths at that point. One of them was what might be described as the road to recovery the other, that of self-doubt. Managing to be on two paths at the same time is of course a conflict, and such are things that stress and depressions are made of.

For the sake of completeness I thought I would just make a comment here about the existing situation. I recognised the current occasion of low mood late in 2015 on the back of a series of deaths of friends and family. I remember telling Dot how I was feeling. She asked whether I was still taking the medication. I told her I'd stopped it some time ago. She said that she really didn't want to see me go through what I had been through before and that I should really start taking the medication again. I did this and it did make a difference. I cannot claim that I am up to scratch, but I am in reasonable control and my mood, whilst still something I would describe as flat, is at least flat at a higher level than it was. I'm also recognising that I may need once again to accept that medication can work and when it does work it's worth keeping on with because my experiences of stopping things have almost invariably resulted in negative symptoms recurring at some point.

Chapter 25 - Where to Guv?

A crossroads in one's life is perhaps an overused metaphor but nonetheless completely appropriate to the situation in which I found myself in the autumn of 2010. I was well aware the average length of time for people staying in work after a diagnosis of Parkinson's is 12 years. I had been working for 16 years and picked up two promotions during that time. I was in a serious job that had a huge element of travel and living away from home. It was also one in which the words that I used in writing my reports had the potential significantly to impact people's lives. This had never been a burden to me. It was instead, a responsibility which I wore with pride. I knew that I now had to face the decision as to whether or not I went back to work at all. The assessment would have to be based on potential, a difficult, perhaps nebulous concept in many ways. Was I likely to fail again? How would anyone judge that? Were there reasonable adjustments that could be made to support me in managing my work? This was worth looking at. Indeed it is a requirement on the organisation to consider. Certainly I knew that work would be more than happy to provide reasonable adjustments if they were feasible. What I didn't want to do was to ask for a series of adjustments for the sake of it which would not then help the core aspect of the job. Given that this core aspect was in fact making judgements about people, it was difficult to see how it would be assisted by any sort of reasonable adjustment. It would still require me to look at and to weigh the evidence and to make a determination based on that.

I knew I had to make some sort of decision and I also knew that I didn't feel capable of doing so alone. I was signed off work but I wanted to be active in dealing with being off work rather than sit quietly waiting for something else to happen and so I pursued the option provided by the civil service of access to support and counselling. The response I got from the support team was really good and very speedy. They could only provide access to counselling as an interim measure subject to me seeking it on a more full-time basis near my home. However, they were able to link me to the counsellor within three days of my phone call. I was entitled to 2 telephone sessions apparently. Not what I would have chosen, I would have preferred face-to-face, but there again needs must and so it was that I agreed to my details being passed on to the counsellor and to be contacted at home.

In some ways, this situation - leave or stay - mirrored that which I faced about leaving grammar school. School was not a great experience for me. Nor was it a dreadful one. Much of my time was spent feeling apprehensive about getting into trouble with another boy or a teacher. I arrived at Xaverian College in September 1966 being 11 years and two or three days old. The first year (called 3a, b and c to complicate matters) was based in a separate building with a separate head teacher, separate play facilities and a separate canteen. We went over to the main school for certain topics such as art, woodwork or music and to access the tuck shop. Otherwise we had lessons in our classroom. This was probably not a bad arrangement for inducting new children into the school where the oldest pupils shaved on a regular basis and were, to all intents and purposes, grown men as far as we were concerned. The majority of teachers were of course perfectly reasonable people. But what stands out and remains fixed in one's mind is a small number who were not reasonable. There is much talk about what goes on in boys' schools and indeed much of it is true. Now I'm not saying that there was gross sexual abuse of boys by anybody at Xaverian but there was a particular master for the first year who had a number of boys he liked to sit on his knee. You have to wonder about that. One chaplain seemed particularly keen on missing one's back when slapping one upon it in a congratulatory manner and instead managing to slap buttocks and rub them at the same time. Later in the school there was a sadistic teacher who delighted in grabbing lads by their sideburns and pulling upwards. I'm not talking about somebody who was dealing with louts who were throwing things around and causing mayhem. Not that it would be the correct response even then. This punishment would be handed out for not paying attention. Completely disproportionate.

There were two teachers who were actively violent and scared me stupid. One, an elderly man who was violent responsively to boys who messed about in class, particularly if he told them more than once to behave. When he went, he went hard. I've seen him lift a desk lid and slam it down on the boy's head on several occasions. And he beat boys across the back with a fist, and banged heads down onto the top of desks. This was a man who may well not have even trained as a teacher given the years I'm talking about but may have come into the profession after military service or as a move from another occupation. He was an expert in his field, but I'm sure that he was not a manager of young men. They got the better of him often which resulted in his outbursts. I don't say this is any excuse but that's something that I could with hindsight at least understand.

The other violent man that I saw was, I think, actually a sadist. This was a young teacher but of course to any of us he was a fully grown adult. He was fit and strong and arrogant in the extreme. Whenever a teacher entered the classroom, we would routinely stand. The majority of teachers would acknowledge us with a 'good morning' and then direct us to sit. This man required us to remain standing. He would then walk up each aisle and randomly punch a boy in the stomach. I have no idea on what he based his decision to punch one boy and not another. If it was his intention to put fear in the class he certainly achieved that with me. I have no idea what was behind his behaviour. He later moved to a girls Grammar School nearby. Rumour has it that he went a step too far with one boy and that this move was the result. Justice indeed. I heard many years later on that he had finally punched a girl and been sacked but I don't know if that's true. Other teachers had very strange ideas about appropriate techniques and methods they might use to get the message over. One I remember used to walk in to class, open his notebook and tell us to 'write this down'. He would then read from his notebook for the full 40 minutes of the lesson and expect us to write down what he said. What an idiot. What a lazy, useless teacher.

So these things stick in one's mind. It's hard to measure the effect they have in the longer term but it's not hard to imagine that they contribute to one's formative development. Throughout my life I have spent many hours pondering the impact of growing up without a father in our family's circumstances. I do not know what the answer is any more than that there is some effect and as an adult I am responsible for managing any negative influence I might be aware of in my behaviour. I do recognise (or at least I think I do) that I have always been slightly wary of meeting a friend's father, particularly for a first-time. Certainly when I was a teenager and even as a young man, I had a certain resistance to engaging with men in authority. It is of course impossible to say whether that would or wouldn't have been different had dad survived. And even if one could make the judgement then the follow-up question of 'to what extent did it play a part' is once again unanswerable. That being said, it served a purpose of helping me to identify and figure out a response to one of the issues that concerned me during those years as I exercise my brain thinking through these questions trying to work up a position on them that I could live with. Learning to think in an organised way and particularly to visualise a route forward from any sort of challenge or difficulty has been an important part of my approach to both work and life in general. Didn't stop me getting ill though.

The saving grace for me at school was music and drama. I was no good at either of them but I did enjoy them both. As far as music was concerned I enjoyed playing and on the drama side I enjoyed the technical aspect rather than performance. The music teacher 'Chuck' Sellars was keen to encourage the orchestra and so there was orchestra practice one evening a week after school and when any event was coming up frequently in lunchtime. What joy, escape from the playground into the warm music room playing either the French horn or the trombone appallingly but energetically.

The school put on some ambitious dramas (in which I include the operas and operettas). As I got older I was a member of the orchestra playing for the shows on a number of occasions.

If I was not involved that way, I liked nothing more than to be involved somehow in the wiring, lighting, sound and scenery or whatever technical aspects I could convince whichever teachers were running the thing to let me loose on. I did appear a couple of times in the first and second year when I was still singing soprano or alto but was much happier from then on to be out of sight and preferably out of mind and left to get on with it.

I could never understand why some boys did not feel anxious about the same things that troubled me. But I guess that's the difference. We are all different in how we learn and how we respond to things that feature in our lives. We mature at different points in time as well, and I am fairly sure I was a later developer. I didn't perform well at Xaverian academically speaking. With hindsight I realise that this is, at least in part, because we weren't taught how to learn, we were taught stuff. As there was an awful lot of it, and I was going through my teenage years so was very distracted by many things. A lot of the stuff fell out of my head and when I sat exams I didn't do well. I also played truant regularly in the fifth form when I should have been working for my 'O' levels. The end result was I passed only three exams with very poor grades which, given the high upon which I had entered the secondary level of the school system, did not reflect well on it or me.

Despite this poor performance, I chose to ask to enter the sixth form and study A-levels. As I look back now I am sure that this was only because I couldn't think of anything else to do, as the expectations were so clear all round. It was in many ways the line of least resistance. I had to ask the head especially for permission to enter because my grades were so poor and rather to my surprise he granted that. That was a bit of a boost, but during the first year in sixth form I didn't feel that I was making any progress. Teaching methods were the same, the distractions on me were the same and the attraction of missing morning lessons because of sleeping were exactly the same.

It had come as a surprise to me when I moved into the sixth form that I was made a prefect. I had absolutely not expected that position to be given to me and had not considered that I would be so identified. This was without question a privileged position at my school, giving both an extra level of autonomy for oneself and authority over pupils throughout the school. There was however no training or preparation available whatsoever and I'm sure I misused the authority I had on more than one occasion. One of the things I didn't do however was truant when I had a prefect duty. My commitment to work and the responsibility of authority shining out even at such a young age. And in fairness, hats off to brother Cyril head of the school who will have been the one who finally decided to award me the role of prefect. Whether it was he who saw my potential that way or that he listened to the views of another I will never know. It certainly helped me to work my way through the rest of sixth form and I think helped me identify a little later in life areas of work that I might not otherwise have considered.

I struggled my way through the two years of the sixth form, growing certainly both physically and emotionally as well as perhaps a little intellectually in that this was, I think, the last aspect of me to mature. Music was my mainstay and although I still played in the orchestra and sang in the choir my real heart was in the folk rock group that I had formed with some friends. We just had the most fun playing music that we enjoyed and only very occasionally playing a gig.

As I expected I screwed my A-levels really badly. The only one I passed was general studies, for which I had not had any lessons, and German 'O' level grade 6. I was cross with myself as well as disappointed and I had no idea what to do. I settled once again for the line of least resistance and asked the head if I could repeat my final year and resit my A-levels. He agreed that I could, but he was a little reluctant and reminded me that I had only scraped into the sixth form at all. I thanked him and returned to school feeling somewhat miffed to be sitting in class with lads from the year below. I thought I'd better try and get stuck in this time and so I did make a bit of an effort in the first couple of months but my heart was definitely not in it. I didn't know where it was but it wasn't where I was physically. The day I realised that I was wasting my time completely was a Friday in early October 1973. It was French. I was sitting in more or less the same place as I had done last year. The teacher was the same teacher that I had for French last year. He read a sentence out of the textbook and proceeded to make exactly the same joke that he had made from exactly the same sentence last year and then laughed in exactly the same way that he laughed last year. Déjà vu! I realised immediately that I had no chance of passing my retakes. Nobody could tell me why I had failed so badly and therefore if they were giving me the same year's tuition I was going to do the same year's study probably (and I knew no better). I was therefore going to fail just as miserably as I had last year. I needed to leave. School was no longer the best place for me to be. But I knew my mum would not be happy.

And I didn't know how to raise the matter with her. I dropped a few hints at home but they were not picked up on. School was the correct place to be; exams were the correct thing to get; going on to university was what I ought to be striving to achieve. I had no argument against these points and anyway hated having rows.

Then out of the blue, tragedy struck as it does, when least expected. A Sunday morning in October 1973, I'm lying in bed aged 18. My brother has married and gone. Mum and Sheila are on the way out to mass and the phone rings. I hear mum answer and I hear her gasp. A moment or two later Sheila appears at my door telling me to get up. Our uncle Owen, our closest and favourite uncle I think, certainly at that time and mum's younger brother, is apparently seriously ill and has been carted off to hospital. Mum and Sheila are going straight around to be with aunty Ursula and I'm to get up and join them as quickly as possible. Just before leaving Sheila said "he's had a heart attack." I heard the door shut and the house felt unbelievably still. I lay in bed and I knew that he was dead.

I can't really remember getting up and getting dressed, nor the 10 or 15 minutes speed walk from our house up into Longsight. I remember the pit in my stomach though, as I turned into their street and saw the cop car outside. So I was right. I hurried to the house and walked in. Aunty Ursula is sitting at the kitchen table clearly shocked and distressed. I don't know what to say or do but I try to adopt as grown up a presence as I can as I know that I need to be useful. My five cousins ranging from Noelle at 18, just four months younger than myself, down to Fiona who was four or five years old had all been sent to church, even though they knew that their dad was not well. I suppose Aunty Ursula was just trying to keep them occupied and give herself some space.

My mum is fussing around the kitchen and the police officer is standing a little awkwardly in front of them both. Somebody is needed to identify the body. Ursula says she can't possibly and mum is very reluctant. During the last summer holidays I had worked as a cleaner at Manchester Royal Infirmary and this included cleaning the mortuary and one time walking in on an autopsy.

"I can do it" I offered. The officer asked my age. "I'm 18" I said. "I've worked in a hospital so I'm fine". In the end it was decided that I would accompany mum, which she felt better about. I can't remember who we left in the house with Ursula apart from Sheila, but there must have been somebody.

The journey to the city mortuary from Longsight is not more than 15 minutes but it was a long, quiet quarter of an hour. The officer led us in and we were shown into a viewing room which had a big window in the side wall and on the other side of that, the curtains were drawn. There was activity in the next room and suddenly the curtains pulled back. There was Owen, covered by a sheet looking terribly unwell. We stood a few moments, heads bowed. There was nothing to say. The formal identification was then completed. His death became an awful reality. He was 46, a husband, the father of five children aged 18 down to 4 and a favourite uncle who called to see us often and I am sure helped mum out significantly. The officer drove us back. My cousins had all returned from church now and all were in a state of stunned shock and disbelief. My mum started to work the telephone, contacting her sisters and breaking the awful news to them. Other people had begun to arrive as is the way at these times. Everything became lost in an air of shock and confusion.

The week following was busy, sad, strange and had an air of finality. I didn't go into school, though in truth I was using the situation as an excuse. Relatives began to arrive to support and some stayed with us, whilst others stayed with Ursula. There was the pleasure of seeing people tarnished by the unhappy circumstance for the meeting. And of course, life goes on. Meals have to be cooked and eaten, shopping bought and dealt with, clothes to be washed and the house to be cleaned. One or more of us were up and down to Ursula's home every day. We tried to engage with our cousins, to distract them for a little while but it was not easy to take their mind off their missing dad. There had to be an autopsy and so the funeral was into the second week after he had died.

One evening I was sitting with my aunty Sheila, mum's older sister, herself a mother of six, who lived in Luton. I can't remember how the conversation started but it turned to my conundrum about school. It was easy to talk to Sheila. Very different than talking to mum. Probably because she wasn't my mum and therefore had a different, perhaps less protective, perspective. I explained the dilemma I felt. One option was following the path of academia which, even though I had shown no evidence of any such ability in my secondary education, I had until very recently expected to be my direction. Another was just leaving school and taking a step into a risky situation where I didn't know what the final destination would be. I explained why I had not felt able to talk about this in any detail to mum and how badly I felt about either staying (for my part) or leaving without repeating my exams (for mum's part). What I heard in Sheila's response was the clear message that ultimately at 18 I had to decide for myself and make my decision by myself. It should be based on my needs and intentions and that whilst it was commendable that I didn't want to upset mum, it was me who would have to live with the consequences of which ever decision I made. This was a surprising message and I guess not the one I had expected to hear but certainly one that I welcomed. In the days since uncle Owen died, I had thought a lot about my dad and the fact that he went out and didn't come back one day. I thought about Uncle Owen and the fact that he got up one morning and that was the end. I thought about wasting another nine months sitting through the same lessons I sat through last year, completing exam papers and then quite likely getting rubbish grades again. And I made a firm commitment to myself that I would leave school. I had no idea what I would do, but I had no intention of just lazing around. I was clear that I would do something.

The funeral came and went. As an extended family we are a close group and although we don't see everybody as frequently as we might like, we all get on really well when we do get together. We never need pallbearers, as there is always a surplus of volunteers to carry the coffin in and out of the church and from car to graveside. I know I carried Owen on at least two of the legs of his final journey. I remember watching my uncle Harry, the senior uncle I suppose, with all three of his children grown up, sobbing in a corner of the house and saying "it should have been me, not Owen". I remember sitting with my cousin Michael the only boy amongst the five children, trying to get him to talk a little bit about how he was

185

feeling. Aunty Phillys kept on urging him to go to the pub with the other men but Michael didn't want to and she started to press him. I had to give her hard word and was a little surprised at myself for being able to. It worked as well and Michael stayed at the house with me, albeit not saying an awful lot.

On the following Monday, resolute if a little raw, I went to school in the morning and instead of going to class went over to the head's office. I explained to him my intention and he wished me well. I think he thought it was probably the best decision anyway. With that I bid him farewell and left.

So I had been in a dilemma. I had to think hard about the options in front of me and needed to have it pointed out to me that this is my life. Whatever I decided to do would have costs and benefits and how I handled them was a matter for me. I had no idea what to do but fortune smiled on me. That night, having left school only a few hours previously, I was round at my friend Stephen's and telling his mum what I had done. She suggested that I join her for the day at the special school where she was deputy head. This was a school for children who were severely mentally handicapped, many of whom would ordinarily have been hospitalised but whose parents were not prepared to agree to that step. I thought it couldn't hurt to go in for a day. I went in for the day and stayed for almost four years.

I did a great deal of growing up during that time. I spent three months going into the Cambrian Unit as it was then called on a daily basis as a volunteer. This was slightly difficult as it meant I had no money coming in and was dependent on mum for my survival. However in the February 1974 I was appointed as a classroom assistant and therefore started to draw a small weekly wage. After about a year of this I moved out of home into a small bedsit room in West Didsbury. This caused quite an amount of tension as I only moved out in order to move out and not because of moving on to anything in particular. But it was what I needed to do. I already learnt to manage my weekly budget, do the washing, the shopping and so forth. But now I was responsible for it entirely. I had fun, I had difficulties, but I learned a great deal more. In addition to all of that, the Unit was the time and the place that I met Dot and married. Funny how life works out. So, that was one crossroads and the twists and turns that took me in a particular direction. A different decision about staying in school, a different outcome no doubt and who knows what life would have been like. But for sure there's no point in worrying about that, brooding on it or indeed having any regrets. I certainly don't. That decision took me down a path that has been filled with experiences, joys, love and of course, sadness. It has brought with it success in many different forms.

And so, back to my current situation: trying to rationalise what is happening to me. I'm an analytical man. I like to understand what's going on. I like to understand the options and possibilities and I need to have some idea of where things are going to lead. I certainly wasn't going to blunder blithely into counselling for the first time in my life assuming either that it was going to be crap or that it would solve my problems. I knew the responsibility lay with me ultimately. Anything that might help me to resolve my issues was worthwhile, whereas anything that tried to take over responsibility was something I needed to be cautious of and indeed perhaps keep a distance from. Anyway, the counsellor's secretary phoned within a week to make arrangements for the telephone contact.

By the time I received the first telephone call from the counsellor, I felt that I had worked out pretty much what it was that was troubling me. It's back to loss again. I define myself as one of Her Majesty's Inspectors of Probation. I know it's not the only role I have. I'm a husband and father, son, brother and so on and so forth. But it was the one I used as a public face. If I was unable to return to work, then potentially I would lose my sense of myself. I would lose my purpose, my raison d'être. I would become useless. I would no longer be a provider. I would be on the rubbish heap. These were the sorts of thoughts I was having and they were not easy ones for me to deal with. The fact of the matter is that although I've had Parkinson's for at least 16 years, and I have always known that it was likely that I would have to finish work early, this had completely taken me aback. I was simply not ready to contemplate these issues, never mind to have sorted them out in my mind and made the appropriate arrangements.

I had been thinking deeply for a couple of weeks about this issue. I recognised that I was looking at a hard reality rather than a series of options and that sometimes hard realities are eased by the simple passage of time. The ability to look ahead takes time to develop but is well worthwhile. The application of an understanding of the stages of grief also played its part. If I was going to lose my main role in life at a time when I wasn't really exercising choice and was being driven by this dreadful illness which I hated with a passion and whose impact I resented more each passing day, then it was a very real loss and it deserved very real attention.

The counsellor telephoned at the appointed time and introduced herself and explained the ground rules on how things would work, all of which I had fully expected and was pleased to hear her say. I knew it was talk therapy for me, playing out the thoughts I had been having about my role and loss and testing out these thoughts on the counsellor. This approach worked very well. She was a quiet listener and summarised what I had been saying each time I paused. This allowed me to hear somebody else's interpretation of what I'd said, to make a judgement as to whether she had got it right or wrong or whether I had perhaps mis-spoken on that thought. Each time that I had spoken to anybody about my situation and the possibility of not returning to work I had become upset. Whilst talking to the counsellor I felt my throat tightening and my chin quivering on a number of occasions and a couple of times I just had to stop talking for a moment. Fortunately she was sensitive enough to recognise what was happening and not to interrupt. At the end of the session I had talked through my concerns and bounced a number of thoughts around about how to manage and what I might need to do to keep some balance in my life so as to ensure that I didn't sit and vegetate. This was never really a high risk but it didn't hurt to be confident and sure that I would be able to do something with my life and make some sort of contribution somewhere instead of walking away from something that was most rewarding to emptiness.

Having said goodbye, after arranging a second contact, I sat for a while thinking. I knew I was moving forward towards accepting the idea of retiring and not feeling like a fraud when saying that I could not manage to do my job any more. Although at any single moment I could feel capable of being at work and doing what was required, it only took a little thought for me to feel very palpably the pressure that I would experience trying to do eight hours never mind a week. Although I was still very unhappy about this reality, I recognised that I was beginning to come to terms with my situation and perhaps was turning the corner towards thinking more positively about using my time and developing my contribution to the world. It was time for a cup of tea and then a walk and some fresh air and exercise. These I did and by the end of that afternoon I was beginning to feel somewhat more hopeful about the future.

Chapter 26 – Due Process

My route into the probation service initially was a circuitous one. One of the key events during my time at the Unit (where I worked after leaving school) was when I spent three weeks during the summer holiday looking after physically disabled children on holiday in North Yorkshire. This was as a volunteer for an organisation that a friend of mine, Mike, worked for. I had not previously worked with physically disabled children and so there was a great deal of learning for me about dressing and physical care as well as mobility issues for this particular group. Unfortunately, during the three-week period Mike had a mental breakdown. I was quite active in trying to minimise the damage that he was causing, albeit inadvertently, as a result of his mental state. Nevertheless, we remained friends and he became better with treatment. He moved to working in the probation service in a recently begun operation called Community Service. This was a new sentence of the court whereby instead of sending an offender to prison, the court ordered them to perform a given number of hours of unpaid work for the benefit of the community. Sentencers loved it and orders were being made quickly. Numbers of such orders grew and the team that had been put together within the Greater Manchester Probation Service was growing rapidly as well.

In mid-1976 Mike invited me to become a sessional supervisor, working on a Saturday, taking a group of adult offenders off to a work site and supervising them at work for eight hours before returning them to the city centre. I was 19 at the time. Somehow I had found my metier. I would have liked to work longer term with the mentally handicapped children but I couldn't survive on the pay and as Dot and I planned to marry in 1977 we needed a better income. Having worked for a year as a sessional supervisor, when Mike moved on to train as a probation officer, I applied for his post as a community service officer. This role involved taking full responsibility for the management of the court order. Although only 21, I was appointed. I worked there for about four years, during which time the scheme continued to grow rapidly. I had responsibility for a caseload of 40 to 50 offenders and also for the recruitment and training of sessional supervisors. I learned a tremendous amount during this time, not only about the ways of organisations, but about other people and about myself. I settled in my heart that I would move on to train as a probation officer as this was something through which I felt I could make a positive contribution.

In 1981, I was interviewed for the Certificate of Qualification in Social Work course at Manchester Polytechnic. In July of that year I was offered a place. At this point Dot was eight months pregnant. Matthew was born in early August. We had been living since our marriage in a flat in Haslingden, Lancashire. This was up four flights of stairs which was no problem at all for us as a couple of young, healthy adults. With the arrival of our beautiful boy it became a challenge, particularly when I returned to work and Dot had to manage the pram and the baby up and down that same four flights of stairs every time she wanted to go out. So we set to, looking for an alternative place to live. We knew the town of Glossop as one of Dot's sisters and her family lived there. It so happened that one of my colleagues also lived there and had a house that she rented out. Her current tenants were due to move out at the end of August and so I quickly seized the opportunity and put down a deposit.

On the Friday of the first week of September 1981, having had a farewell non-alcoholic drink with my teammates, I drove my car to the van hire depot, and picked up the three ton vehicle that I had booked. I drove to our home in Haslingden and started carrying our belongings down the now famous four flights of stairs to the van. My good friend Wasyl, had offered to help. He managed to arrive at about 8:30pm, at which point the van began to fill up rather more quickly. We took the first load at about midnight and over the rest of Saturday we made another couple of trips and took the final items very late on Saturday night. The last journey involved dropping Matthew at my mum's house, taking Dot to the house in Glossop, returning the van to the depot, picking up the car, driving to my mum's, putting Matthew onto the back seat in his carrycot and driving to the new house. I spent the journey listening for him to make noises and had to stop on four occasions to check that he was still breathing. No new parent nerves for me then! Sunday was spent having a walk around Glossop and putting various things away to make living easier. On the Monday morning I set off for the Manchester Polytechnic campus in East Didsbury for the induction week for my probation officer training course. My poor course colleagues - they were all keen to get to know one another given that we would then spend the next two years together - had to put up with me being quite frankly not the least interested in them but boasting all the time about my new baby son. I find it difficult to remember having that much energy. I know that the passage of time has its effect on all of us and my Parkinson's adds to that, but it would be nice still to have a moderate percentage of that level to keep me going.

The course was the required qualification for all social workers and probation officers. Probation officers achieved their qualification by taking the course along with the probation option, whilst social workers would pick childcare or work with the elderly as their specialist option. My position was funded by the Home Office and so I could afford to take the course and keep the family just about fed and clothed for the two years, after which time it was up to me to find a position with a probation area as a qualified probation officer.

It had been a long time since I had studied, but I had wanted to take this course for some time and I was very committed to passing it and to do well. Partly, I think this was my way of recovering my sense of myself. I had got a little lost academically during school years. The two years of the course was spent in blocks of study at the Polytechnic along with blocks of practice in a variety of fieldwork settings. For a while, I worked as a social worker in Ashton. I had a placement at Manchester prison for a few weeks. This was a fantastic opportunity that one would not wish to experience any other way than on a placement. The chance to walk around the wings talking to prisoners and staff was invaluable in terms of the work I was planning to do. For the final six months of the course I worked as a probation officer in Hyde, part of the Greater Manchester Probation Area, for whom I had worked whilst in the community service team.

During that last six months of the course I had to apply for posts as a probation officer and I duly applied to Greater

Manchester and was awarded a place on a waiting list. During that time we also had to write a thesis or extended essay as part of the course assessment. I chose to write about the Role of the Pre-sentence Report in the Sentencing Process and was delighted to be awarded 70% which was the highest mark in the whole of the group and the equivalent of a first-class. This helped my sense of myself no end.

Once the course came to an end, which was effectively at the end of the examinations in May I had to wait for a place to come available within Greater Manchester and I would be allocated from the waiting list. There was no guaranteed timeframe for this and so I had to sign on for unemployment benefits for the first time in my life.

By this time, May 1983, Richard had been born. Between then and October when I started work as a qualified probation officer in Salford, we had, as a family, an oddly testing time.

Matthew was 21 months old and had to undergo an operation. This was to be done at Booth Hall hospital in North Manchester a long way from where we lived. Richard was three months old and Dot had had a couple of difficult discussions with health visitors about the fact that he didn't appear to smile very much. It was true, but it wasn't the case that he didn't smile at all and they wouldn't elaborate on their concerns. Eventually our concerns took us along to the clinic to ask them to conduct an eye test. This they did challenging us as to why we have not attended sooner as they had asked us to (to which we replied that they had never said what they wanted us to return for). As a result, an urgent referral was made for Richard to the ophthalmology department of Tameside Hospital.

In some ways it was useful that I had finished my course and had not yet been appointed as a probation officer. The next thing to happen, which one would never have planned for, was that our Austin Allegro car was sideswiped by an idiot pulling into the traffic after coming out of a pub. Although the damage looked small, it had impacted the steering as well as the suspension and bodywork and the car was inevitably written off.

Richard's appointment came through very quickly. We made the journey by bus. It takes about 25 minutes in the car during the day to get from our home to the local hospital and an hour and a half by bus. We left Matthew at his cousin's house to play and the other 3 of us took public transport, both Dot and I with dry mouths and anxious stomachs. Richard of course, just slept. We were not kept waiting long when we were called into the orthoptist's consulting room. She was a young woman, well-spoken and smartly dressed. But as she was organising us into the various places she wanted us she called me "daddy". This did not go down well and I made my views clear, including telling her that I was nowhere near old enough and gave her a couple of options to call me Ray or Mr Wegrzyn. This caused a little tension but we got past it soon enough thankfully. She waved various things in front of Richard's face and peered at him through a variety of lenses and then said that she wanted the consultant ophthalmologist to assess him as well. We all trundled along to his clinic and it was the consultant himself who took Richard and peered into his eyes with a series of lenses and lights.

The professionals spoke to each other in a huddle and we were escorted back to the first room. We were told bluntly that Richard had a condition called nystagmus, and that this was usually associated with severe mental handicap. This was shocking news. It also turned out that the health visitors had thought he was blind and to this day I have no idea why they felt they could not have a sensible discussion with us rather than trying to patronise us with their professionalism. I am confident that things have changed in their culture.

We were also told that Richard would have poor vision, but this seemed barely relevant in the context of all we have been told. The journey home by bus was not an easy one. Tears were brimming and minds blank. We collected Matthew and went home, both of us not really able to believe that this gorgeous little blond haired boy could be severely mentally handicapped or even mildly so. This was not to do with any irrational prejudice as we had both worked with severely handicapped children. It was instead, our recognition of his responsiveness, albeit perhaps less overt than in many children. We knew that only time would tell and we would have to wait on this, but in the meantime, we had some concrete things to do to stimulate his vision's responses and we could get on with that straight away.

The next day however, a letter landed advising us that Matthew was on the list for his operation the following week. We had to attend Booth Hall Hospital on the Tuesday morning very early, and the operation would be performed that day. Now getting to Booth Hall Hospital without a car is a bigger challenge than I wanted to deal with particularly with both of the children plus things for Dot to stay over in the hospital. This also of course meant Richard had to stay there as Dot was breastfeeding. I decided to hire a car and bill the insurance of the fool who had written off the Allegro. So we hired an orange Ford Fiesta which meant that we would be able to get to the hospital relatively smoothly and that I would be able to visit back and forth at appropriate times and not depend on public transport timetables. We were clear that Dot would stay in hospital with Matthew. We would not leave him there at 22 months old without one of us and as she doesn't drive, it needed to be she who stayed. I had made contact with the hospital and they had indicated no problem with this apart from the fact that Dot might have to use a couch.

Disappointingly, on arrival we met a rather different response which included a reluctance to have Richard staying and an absolute inability to provide Dot with a cot for him. We decided to play a long game rather than argue there and then but Dot was as determined as anyone could be in terms of protecting her children and she was not going to have either Richard go hungry or Matt be alone. Enough said.

The operation took place and Mathew duly came round and was returned to his cot on the ward. He has always been a very happy chap, and he loved taking his medicine, to the extent that the nurses seemed to enjoy giving it to him. It was a real battle with many children. Dot spent most of the week with him and Richard in the hospital, working her way around the nurses some of whom were fantastically helpful but some of whom were clearly non-commissioned officers in the awkward squad. They met their Commander-in-Chief. I travelled back and forth and one night having arrived home rather late from the hospital I was sitting in the living room when I heard a bang outside. I went out to find that a chap had reversed his car into my hire car and was trying to drive away. I remonstrated with him and took down his number. He was rude and argumentative, goodness knows why, as I wasn't even in the car, but I decided because of the attitude as much as anything else, that I would report him to the police. The station was just down the road and I went and did that immediately, giving them all the information I could. He turned out to be the brother of our elderly neighbour with whom we got on extremely well and she was mortified, but not surprised, at her brother's behaviour. Needless to say I lost my deposit on the hire car. This was made the more galling some six months later as I was walking past the garage and saw the car there. It had the exact dent that had been caused during my hire of it and for which I had lost my deposit. I was glad when I heard that the man responsible had been put before the court and fined, albeit nothing ever got my way in terms of costs.

So, between having successfully completed my training to become a probation officer and taking up my first professional post I was fairly well challenged on a number of fronts. Between us, Dot and I, carrying our two little men with us, met these adversities head-on and battered them as they deserved. Happily, apart from the nystagmus and low vision, the medics were entirely wrong about Richard who like his older brother has grown up a bright, capable, well-balanced, mature young man. It could easily have been so different.

My work as a probation officer began in the October that year and took me initially to Salford, where I worked as a main grade officer supervising a full range of case types. The first year in practice is, quite properly, very carefully supervised. Checks are made on work on a regular basis by the team manager and three times during the first year by the area manager. I seemed to be viewed as meeting expectations and showing the willingness to take on work. Areas of practice were highlighted where I needed to make changes. That first year passed very quickly and it was probably only nine months until I was starting to move towards working for a while with the specialist juvenile justice team in Salford. That was one of those little groups of people that works extremely well together because they all share standards of practice and maintain an active debate about methods to improve outcomes.

By 1987, when I was considered to be well experienced, I applied for and took on a specialist role as a crime prevention worker. I worked on an estate for a period of time as part of a Home Office project. This included working in partnership with the neighbourhood police team, in particular with the sergeant of that team, Nigel Bonson who was a similar age to myself and who had an excellent perspective which meant we worked together - we both thought - extremely well. Whether we had any measurable impact on the behaviour of the young people on the estate is a matter for others to determine. What we did show was that people from the different agencies can work together effectively if they think about what they're doing and apply themselves to purpose as well as process. I learnt a tremendous amount from this posting and particularly from working with the police which stood me in good stead in later years working with more senior officers in partnership working, as well as joint inspection work.

I became one of four senior probation officers in Oldham in early 1990. I managed the court team and the probation supervision team and had districtwide responsibility for administration and the admin staff. I was also responsible for anything to do with court work and jointly ran district-wide meetings and other projects as appropriate. After four years in Oldham, I took on the local management of a major project being run by the Home Office to implement some new information systems. The issues here are covered earlier in the book. This is where I start to become alert to the fact that my body was not quite performing as it ought to and had been doing. Despite the health issues I completed my secondment which coincided very well with a vacancy for a position as the district manager for probation back in Salford. In February 1998 I took up the reins at Salford probation this time running the whole operation with over 90 staff. This was undoubtedly my best posting so far. I thoroughly enjoyed the role and was more than happy to be responsible as long as I had the authority to make decisions. I was very active in the multi-agency strategic planning groups that existed around several areas of significant criminality and other antisocial behaviours. Finally, in February 2002, I was delighted to be appointed as one of Her Majesty's Inspectors of Probation. This started as another secondment, but after three years I was given the opportunity of returning to my service or becoming a permanent civil servant and I chose the latter, which turned out to be an excellent decision.

Chapter 27 – The end in sight

So I found myself in 2010 at 55 years of age off work sick and seriously considering whether I could return. At one level this was momentous. At another simply a bureaucratic process. My reality I guess, would be somewhere in the middle.

During my first few weeks off, I did very little. I was taking antidepressants as prescribed and thinking a great deal. I recognised that, at the back of my mind, the issue of retirement was floating about and that I wasn't taking it seriously at this stage. Rather I was thinking about how I could get back to work in a reasonable timeframe and not get into the same difficulties that had brought me to this point. I thought about the fact that I was regularly falling asleep whilst involved in file reading and more recently struggling to stay awake during meetings. I was very aware that people were noticing this, although fortunately nobody has yet raised the issue either with me or as a complaint. I would have been mortified. I was unhappy with myself about this particular aspect of my life whether it was within my control or not. All my reading suggested not, but there was still a little nagging doubt in the back of my mind on that point.

One of the hardest things to address was the fact that I felt anxious about my work. It wasn't that I didn't know how to do anything, it was that I just felt I wasn't going to do a good job. I suppose it was my confidence that was lacking and again I have found this to be a common feature amongst people with Parkinson's. I didn't know how to build up my confidence other than by doing that which I felt worried about doing. The risks involved in that however were high, because if I failed, it could be a very visible outcome and could have a bearing on the Inspectorate as a whole, something I was simply not prepared to risk.

All these thoughts kept pointing towards retirement as the right direction. My still uncertain and mixed up emotional thoughts also told me that people would consider me to be swinging the lead and just looking for an easy way out of work. Nothing could in fact be further from the truth. I would give up having Parkinson's at the drop of a hat if that were possible. Indeed, I'd be willing to pay for the privilege. I would then continue working until my true retirement date with a big grin plastered to my face. This was another example of my Catholic guilt running riot right or wrong and my conscience pricking me, affected by emotion rather than sense or logic.

I knew enough from my training and practice about using visualisation techniques as a way of working through situations in advance and I also knew the benefit of having discussions with a range of people and just trying out ideas on them to see what sort of responses came back. Thus the topics of my conversations over a few weeks with a number of people (who shall remain nameless here but you know who you are folks and thanks) were Parkinson's, employment and what Ray should do about his current situation. I talked to people about the effects of the condition. In particular the hidden symptoms, the non-visible things that have such a powerful and draining effect on most of us with the condition. Some of the reactions from people surprised me. Friends that I had talked to quite openly but had never mentioned for example, that hallucinations were a common side effect of some of the medication and that I experienced them, expressed absolute shock at the fact that I was having to put up with those. Another was horrified to hear about the active sleep disorder and my leaping around and punching walls. These were things that I was very used to by now and no longer found shocking or surprising and so it was helpful to hear these reactions and thus recognise the value of being clear with people about these hidden symptoms.

I also engaged people in discussions about being retired, particularly the financial implications, but most of all the implications for one's sense of self. I had many really helpful discussions, some with people who knew what I was doing and joined in heartily. Other genuine discussions were with people who didn't know I had any subtext but were just engaging with me in terms of whatever I was saying. All of these were hugely helpful in enabling me to sort out the knots that were tied up in my brain. None of them gave me the answer. Of course, I knew they wouldn't. That was my responsibility. But at the same time, I longed for somebody to tell me what to do.

A magnificent distraction during this particular time was the forthcoming wedding of our younger son Richard to his fiancée Jen. They had planned a grand day between them and I was hugely flattered to have been asked to speak at the wedding ceremony. Public speaking is not something that I have any particular problem with. At least didn't have any particular problem with. The more I thought about what I might say the less I was sure that I should be saying anything. I began to get myself into a bit of a tizz and Richard picking up on this phoned me one evening to say "don't worry about it dad. You don't have to say anything. We're happy that you be there. And I certainly don't want the idea of saying something at my wedding to cause you any more stress or make you feel unwell". I could have cried – so I did, just a little bit. That conversation made me take a deep breath, look at my track record, remember some of the public speaking I have done, and set to with vigour to write a piece that was both sensitive, pointed and appropriately humorous. I did this around the theme of families joining together. This was all well and good until I saw the draft remarks that the registrar was due to make which talked about families coming together and other topics that I had put in my speech. A quick redraft was called for and I realised that I needed actually to think of a new theme. I moved to the one about making the big decisions and the small decisions and importance of both. I did my usual preparation of writing it out in narrative format and then speaking it out loud to hear where it didn't work and where I needed to punctuate or change words. There were a whole series of edits to get it just how I wanted and within the time that was indicated. I'm delighted to say it was delivered as written and by all accounts well received at the event. I was certainly a proud man that day, as well as having had a thoroughly good time.

Excellent distraction though it was, in a few days, I was back struggling with making a decision about my situation. What were the implications if I were to retire? Financially I would probably not do too badly as the civil service pension is a good one. I had also taken out an Advance Voluntary Contribution policy shortly after being diagnosed on the basis that I was likely to have to stop work early at some point. If it was the case that I could get a pension we could live on reasonably, without me having to earn some money to supplement the pension, then that would be a good situation. If I did earn money it would be a luxury. However I had questions about the pension documentation that I received and needed to look into it. If I were to stay at work, then obviously my income would increase. The work itself would continue to be as it had been for the past eight years. This was where I was going around in circles. I needed to be stopped and required to make a decision. I was finding it so ridiculously difficult and this is where I kept falling down. I could not see any way of enabling me to manage that seemingly simple requirement. I thought about all the possible reasonable adjustments I have ever heard of. These included a half-time personal assistant, but the job simply did not lend itself to that arrangement. It was so difficult to identify how anything could help me with the things with which I was struggling; the time it was taking me to think about what I was assessing, the problem of staying awake during the course of the working day. Nor could I see any way of managing on reduced hours either. Every time I sat down to think about these difficult issues, I ran into a dead-end.

In the middle of this mixed up period of time, I had an appointment at the hospital to see the neurologist for a routine follow up. I had decided that I would talk to the doctor about the work situation. I had also decided that I would visit my office after my appointment. It was only ten minutes from the hospital. It was likely to be fairly quiet and it would be an opportunity for me to test out how contact with work affected me. The last time I had visited which was only a week or so after I had gone sick, I had ended up sitting in my car bawling my eyes out after having been in there for only an hour. I couldn't explain then why I had that reaction nor can I now.

But I needed to check out that it wasn't something that was likely to happen again.

Despite asking, I was not able to see Dr Dick and so once again was seen by one of the Registrars. With the exception of Dr Dick whom I've seen on three of my visits, it has been a different doctor each time. Of course they're all focused on Parkinson's at that point in their career but it doesn't seem to me to be quite the same as having a view from an expert. I reported all my symptoms to the Registrar as I did on each occasion and highlighted those which were the most problematic to me. He was a young man with a very good personal style. He was clearly listening to me and thinking about his explanations and answers. Once we got through the potential changes to my medication regime I raised the issue of work with him, interested to see what he would say. Pretty much as I had expected he said it was difficult for him to comment as he didn't really know me but on the whole work was a good thing. Of course, if it was creating such stress as to be worsening the symptoms of the condition, that would be different. But when that tipping point was reached was a matter for each individual to determine. Fair enough and certainly by no means was he saying "there's no way that you're not fit mate". Equally he wasn't saying "time you jacked it in lad".

Chapter 28 - Resolution

At around this time, and certainly whilst still sitting on my dilemma's horns, I had also decided that I would apply for a blue disabled parking badge under the local scheme. This was because my walking had become quite badly affected and I was certainly struggling getting out of my car and on many occasions actually walking any distance at all was hard work. I used a stick all the time and felt lost without one. This was connected with a sense of imbalance that I had been experiencing, not at all like an ear based balance problem, rather a feeling of weakness and lack of physical control. I had difficulty in getting on with the application because I wasn't convinced that I met the definition given in the documentation for eligibility. I spoke to a number of friends who had badges all of whom said that I was more than eligible and why didn't I just get on and apply. Catholic guilt strikes again. Finally, I decided to fill the forms in and drop them down at the doctor's surgery for their processing. I was confident that I had written up my application truthfully and my GP knew me well enough to have a view as to whether I met the criteria or not. I was told it would take 2 to 3 weeks and that I would hear either way. I saw this as something of a trial. If I was not awarded a blue badge that was an assessment I could fully accept and which would be telling me what a number of experienced people, some of whom knew me quite well thought about my situation. Equally if I was granted a blue badge then I was officially a disabled person and that brought with it some softening of my resistance. It took the full three weeks for the answer to land on the doorstep and it was, rather to my surprise, 'yes'. The blue badge was enclosed along with an explanation as to how it was to be applied. I felt very strange indeed. On one hand this was a clear statement of positive support for me by some knowledgeable people who not only knew me but also knew the context within which these decisions were made. On the other hand it was a clear statement by that same group of knowledgeable people that I was disabled and had difficulties. I felt befuddled.

I continued thinking and talking, keeping as up to date as I could and engaging a range of people to bounce ideas and thoughts off. It finally ended with a discussion with my GP. I had been trying to get to see him but he is difficult to find appointments with and so I arranged a telephone consultation to agree a number of changes in my medication with him, following my trip to hospital and the letter from the Registrar I had seen there, outlining his proposals. At the end of the discussion I asked my GP whether he had was prepared to give me a further sick note. His answer took me by surprise. He said not only was he prepared to write me one he was going to make it out for three months. He said that this was to signal to my employers how serious he thought my situation was. Furthermore he was going to write not only depression but also deteriorating Parkinson's disease. He then went on to say that in his considered opinion, his unequivocal advice to me would be that I should retire. I was a little surprised as I had expected him to be taking a fairly neutral position much like the hospital Registrar, although of course he did know me better. When I expressed some surprise at his definitive statement he commented that he had seen me around town and at the surgery and of course had experience of people in similar situations.

The timing of this conversation was quite helpful as I was due to have my first meeting with Liz, my boss, a couple of days later as part of the management of sickness absence procedures. Having my GP's opinion so resolutely expressed helped me to have more confidence in my own thinking.

Chapter 29 - Mixing

Outside my work role I am by nature a rather shy man. I don't find it particularly easy to mix socially and tend to avoid going to events where the ability to small-talk and manage to handle a plate of food and a glass of drink at the same time is de rigueur. There are a number of reasons for this. Being a teetotaller is one of them, not that it's a big issue these days. People are used to it particularly since the tightening up of drink-driving laws. But when you're the only one who is always stone cold sober it can get a bit tedious watching other people get merry on a couple of glasses of wine. Truth be told, Parkinson's hasn't helped with this. I am more self-conscious because of my tremor and other physical movement difficulties and still unsure how to deal with explaining things on first meeting people. My natural tendency is to be fairly blunt, but that sometimes has the effect of stopping things in their tracks, which isn't always what you want to achieve. Such reactions have caused me to hold back from getting into the situation in the first place. Deafness also certainly features in keeping me away from events where there will be a lot of background noise. Even though I have modern digital hearing aids which are very good at enhancing sound, they can't filter the way the human ear can and so I find it increasingly difficult to hold reasonably quiet conversations with people when there is a hubbub in the background, which is so common these days. But truth be told, I have always struggled in social settings and remember that I felt uncomfortable as a child with any new circumstance. I think this just continued into adult life and although I can control it more logically, emotionally I just want to operate in small groups of family or friends, or indeed, on my own.

I have always been an active computer user since buying my very first one - an Amstrad dual disc machine. I have learned by experimentation and enjoy the Internet as much as anybody. It was a few years after diagnosis that I discovered that there were a number of forums on the Internet for people with Parkinson's. They served the purposes of support and information sharing and there was of course a common basis for everybody who visited the sites. It was easy enough to decide to join one or two of them and I learned a tremendous amount by reading the postings of other people who had the condition. From there I discovered the Young Parkinson's network. Young in Parkinson's terms means anybody diagnosed under 40. Some readers may be surprised to know that there are approximately 6000 people in the UK who are diagnosed under the age of 40.

I recognised that many of the postings were from people who sought company. There were also a considerable number of people who were looking for information from other people rather than from official sources. Although I was happy to learn a great deal from reading other members postings I always checked everything I was wanting to pursue against written scientific material. This, to my mind is simply good practice and in line with my normal way of doing things, neither better nor worse than anybody else's way of doing things. However it did mean that I was very cautious about posting unless it was on some topic about which I was absolutely confident. So although I was recognised as a visitor to a number of forums, I was not particularly well known nor did I get to know any of the other contributors other than via the forum.

In more recent years I have become aware that people who meet on forums often get together for support and socialising. This again had mixed appeal. Sharing the experience of Parkinson's clearly has the potential to help both myself and anybody else that I talk with. Equally, meeting up with people involves being sociable and I have explained some of my difficulties with that.

I had seen postings from a young woman called Becky who was diagnosed at the age of 29. She subsequently gave birth to her first child. My heart went out to her, being diagnosed with such an illness at such an early point in her life. At least I had got up to 39 with my children doing well and facing the right direction and my career fully established. She wrote passionately about her desire to contribute to the development of a cure for Parkinson's by raising money to fund research for that specific purpose. On the forum that I frequented most of the time, she mooted the idea of a black-tie ball to raise funds and asked members for active support in making that happen. The response was at best muted. For me it was silent for the reasons that I've expounded. After a while she clearly got fed up and made her feelings known and stopped visiting that particular site. It was not unusual for people to stop attending sites and no particular comment was made.

Some months later, whilst exploring a different site, I noticed her name and decided to have a look at her postings. They were still about a black-tie ball but as I read through them I realised that it was a reality and it was due to happen at a prestigious location in the Midlands with a deal with a local hotel for people to stay over and lots of media coverage and involvement of celebrities. I was impressed and pleased for her in a distant kind of way. I was pleased that she managed to get some support for her idea and turn it into a reality. I wasn't particularly bothered about a black-tie ball and had no idea how these things work or how much money it could raise.

Still an impressive feat. A few weeks later we happened to be online at the same time and she struck up a conversation. I'm better at responding than initiating and so I did reply and the conversation soon came round to the ball. I mentioned to her that I had been on the previous forum when she had initially mooted the idea and congratulated her on getting it developed. Over the next few weeks we chatted occasionally about general matters and I realised that she was an intelligent and capable woman who had some good ideas and an amazing amount of drive. She had a commitment to fundraising and was prepared to put the effort in to achieve her goals. This gave me some food for thought. At this point I had lived with Parkinson's for well over 10 years during which time I had looked after myself and pretty much avoided engaging with anybody else who have the condition. I certainly had not had any dealings with any charity apart from being sponsored to do a 100 foot abseil down the outside of the Manchester town Hall. Whilst this was set up to raise money for Parkinson's I did it for the thrill and I make no bones about it.

Chatting again with Becky one evening she expressed great concern at having to give a speech at the ball which was due to happen in about four weeks' time. I was surprised at this admission and challenged it. She was a well-educated, multilingual professional with the confidence to put her ideas on the table and keep working at other people until they went along with her. Surely she could say a few "thank you's" to people. Well, yes, she admitted that she could, but she wanted to give a speech and that was the point. She could say a few "thank you's" which might sound a bit dreary when she wanted to make a speech that would motivate people to spend money which was of course the object of the exercise.

With my recent thinking about helping others and fundraising banging on in my head I, rather foolishly perhaps, offered to write a speech for her. She protested that she couldn't possibly ask me to do such a thing and I pointed out that I had offered, she hadn't asked. Anyway, I was more than happy to draft something for her. She admitted that it would be a weight off her mind and so I undertook to provide her with some thoughts within a few days.

This was much more my cup of tea. I sat down and mind mapped a series of elements that such a speech ought to contain: thanks; a reminder of the purpose of the event; an explanation of where the event fitted into any context; and a prompt to spend money. She had told me that she only had five or six minutes and I had made enough speeches to know both how much and how little you can say in that period of time as well as the tendency of the nervous deliverer to speed up, sometimes to as much as double the correct rate of speech.

I drafted out a version of the speech including a range of superlatives, using some alliteration and metaphor, and lots of personal touch. I knew that Becky was married and had one child and that her husband looked after the home and both of them very well indeed. I knew that members of her family would be present. Her employer had been hugely supportive as had various members of staff from the Cure Parkinson's Trust, the charity to which any profits would go. These all would be thanked. I wrote a very personalised "woman on a mission" speech and sent the draft over. I was quite amazed at the positive response, having expected considerably more change than was in fact requested. Those changes that were requested were done so hesitatingly as if putting a burden on me but as I pointed out I wanted to deliver a good product so that she could deliver a good speech.

On the night in question I was delighted to learn that her dad had recorded her delivering the speech along with a poem that she had written which came at the end. I thought it was very well delivered. There was appropriate emotion and various pauses for applause. There was laughter at a couple of places and overall it was delivered with feeling. I was chuffed to have made a contribution. The ball made £30,000 clear profit all of which went to the Cure Parkinson's Trust. A very impressive achievement by a young woman battling a debilitating illness but not willing to give in to the dictatorship of Parkinson's.

The ultimate outcome of this collaboration and new friendship, albeit one based on a shared sense of siege, was that we jointly wrote a collection of poetry. This was enhanced by some artwork by Ghislaine Howard, a friend of mine from Glossop who is a nationally renowned artist. Her mother also lives with Parkinson's.

Chapter and Illuminating Verse was well received by those who read it. We received many positive comments. I never worked out a good marketing strategy for it, and so there are still copies available from me.

Chapter 30 - this is the BBC. Stay calm and keep talking

Where would we be without our friends? For me, that can and does include members of my extended family. I often wonder what people who were friends of mine before I became unwell think and whether or not they see me differently than those relatively few people that have become friends since I was diagnosed. For me without doubt, Parkinson's is a standard topic of conversation as it affects me and how I feel every day and all the time. Occasionally I wonder if I'm overstating its impact as far as others are concerned. Many of my closest friends are clearly concerned to see the effect on me recently and have begun to find out for themselves a little more about the condition. It is hard to find the words to explain how much this is appreciated. The friendship it demonstrates often has me in sombre contemplation when I'm alone. You cannot put a price on such generous use of self and time.

In light of a conversation about such matters during one of the board meetings for the charity I set up, (more about that shortly) Tom made a link with the Radio 4 programme called the Listening Project. This is part of the development of a verbal archive held at the British Library. Two people are recorded having a conversation about anything. The edits are very short, less than five minutes in length and some are broadcast on Radio 4. It took little discussion to agree that we should have a go at being recorded. Tom took on the job of getting in touch with the programme makers and finding out what we would need to do to be recorded. We also thought maybe we could have a 4 way conversation about the charity.

Tom sent an email and in due course received a very positive response inviting him to contact a particular person for a brief telephone chat. That was essentially to clarify that the programme realty was about two person conversation and that the dynamics of 3 or 4 way chats did not really work the same. This made reasonable sense and so we decided to press ahead with two, one of whom, the other trustees insisted, had to be me.

So it was that on 23 June 2015, Tom and I rolled up to BBC radio Midlands to meet with Mark Newman, the producer of the Listening Project in that region. He was very relaxed and personable and spent an hour talking us through all aspects of the recording and the aftermath and explained clearly that the decision to broadcast was made by others and depended on a number of factors that we would not know such as the topics that had recently been broadcast. Nevertheless, the recording would go into the national archive and we could also have a copy ourselves. We knew we would put this on our website and were keen to receive our copy.

Once we got started on the general topic of what happens to friendships when one of the friends gets ill and dynamics change, Tom and I talked for a full hour. I knew we would because that's we do but it was good that it could happen in the rather different environment of the BBC recording studio. We felt happy enough with what we could recall we had said and went off looking forward to receiving the different edits from the producer.

As I write now in early June 2016 we have finally received the edits after a long delay and some chasing and we are waiting to find out whether or not the short edits will be broadcast. The full recording is about 53 minutes and then we have two shorter ones that would be suitable for broadcasting if the content is also suitable. Eventually, the full broadcast will end up on our website. It's quite fascinating the way that the radio producer can take 53 minutes with the recording and extract and refit cogent sections that still have a degree of completeness. Still, others may judge if it's broadcast or if they listen to it on the website.

For a variety of reasons, none of which matter particularly, there were difficulties in setting the recording initially on the BBC Radio West Midlands system and then subsequently on the national archive at the British library. This required considerable liaison with Mark Newman in order to get the matter attended to. I was delighted to receive an email last week telling me that after almost 3 years, all the technical issues had now been sorted out and the recordings were live on both databases.

It's a fact of course, that some waits are worthwhile. Shortly after receiving this email I got a telephone call from a woman who works for radio 4 to tell me that the listening project programme broadcast on radio four nationally was going to broadcast our recording. This transmission would probably be at the end of April or early May, which gives us plenty of time to let people know about it. I was surprised that this was happening at all, given how long it had taken to get things organised technically. However, we are in a much better position to maximise the use we can make of such exposure to the overall benefit of our charity and therefore to a number of people living with Parkinson's.

Chapter 31 - Near the final straight

And so I have been assessed by colleagues and managers, by nurses and doctors, by occupational health and pensions advisors, by family and friends and by support workers from a variety of sources. I have been asked about walking, balancing, shaking, falling, toilet habits, bedtime habits, night-time habits, sex, slurring, drooling, and swallowing. I have had to describe myself at my worst without the benefit of drugs. I'm too frightened to go completely without medication and apart from the research sessions I have no actual experience of this. I can only extrapolate from the low level that I get to occasionally to describe what this state is like. All of this has been done with good intention by kind and capable people who have no inclination at all to see me struggle. They ask questions to ensure I get the right benefit or the correct worker or the correct medication or the correct advice, support and guidance. They consider me to be deserving of their inputs and I in return am truly grateful for their concern and consideration.

The process of requesting retirement on grounds of ill-health is a little fuddled I think. First of all I had not expected it to be something I had to apply for but rather something that work would expect me to accept. Once I had phoned personnel about the matter I received a form to complete which I did as usual to the best of my ability. I was not clear what the process would be after that. However it did identify to me that there were two levels of health retirement the higher level being full access to a topped up pension as if one had worked until that point had been reached. The lower level was retirement with access to the pension only up to the point at which you were in fact at. I had a few years to go until my pension would be at its maximum and so it made quite a difference. The other point that I gleaned from the paperwork and so on was the implication that a lower level suggested that it might be possible to return to work at some point.

As well as filling in paperwork the process required me to be assessed by an occupational health doctor. This involved a trip into Manchester to meet with an extremely pleasant consultant who was very generous with his time and very supportive of my application. He clearly had some understanding of Parkinson's and at the end of the discussion he expressed the view that there were no options for me other than retirement and that in his view continuing to work was not feasible.

I was surprised and disappointed when I received the lower level permission to retire because of my health and immediately made some enquiries as it certainly had not been mine nor my bosses' expectation. I didn't get to see any of the paperwork that had been submitted and so don't know what was written in the occupational health consultant's report. However it clearly wasn't sufficient in one way or another to convince the pension assessor of my situation.

I discovered that the firm had made no attempt to get information from my neurologist. Apparently, that was up to me to do, but that hadn't been made clear. There was an appeals process however, and I decided straight away to follow that. I contacted Dr Dick's secretary who was immensely helpful. I explained that I wanted a letter from Dr

Dick to the pension assessor explaining that Parkinson's was as it is and confirming that I did indeed have the condition. I was also prepared to attend any panel or individual for assessment if necessary. Dr Dick was both willing and reluctant. He was willing to provide the information but had never been asked for it by the applicant before. I gather that he had only ever been asked to provide that sort of information by an employer. When I reassured him that I was happy that this was what I needed to do and I wasn't being manipulated he agreed to do it at a reduced fee which I thought was a very kind thing for him to do.

The appeal process went in my favour at the first point. It seems clear that the letter from Dr Dick had done the job and I was mightily relieved as the financial difference this made was not inconsiderable.

I found it very difficult to believe that I could no longer work, and that I no longer work because I am not physically capable of doing a job that I have loved for so long and which I have done sufficiently well to feel proud of my contribution and achievement.

I spent time thinking about how I might spend time as a retired person. I have no intention at all of being a TV watcher and will be busy as indeed I have been since stopping work. Music, writing, socialising, enjoying the area in which we live, all fill time for me. A weeks' worth of diary is quickly filled up with these few things. It's very important for me to remember that I don't have to do any of them or any that I do, need not be done permanently. I can choose to start or stop doing something. So it's different than work but it can be as satisfying, productive and rewarding as work if indeed not more so on occasion. And I will be paid for it by pension, guilt or not.

With Parkinson's and its heavy toll on physical movement, I'm very well aware that I have to keep moving and keep practising in order to keep my movement accessible for longer. Equally I know that I'm not going to win that battle either and that one day I might lose my ability to walk to such an extent that I may need a wheelchair. I may lose my ability to make the finger patterns required on the saxophone, but at least I will have achieved my ambition of learning to play one. I contemplate losing my ability to do my job. I've been blessed with having work that I have always enjoyed. Yes, I found it challenging but equally it has been fully rewarding. In my last role as an inspector I made a small difference on a national scale. That's not bad for a lad from Victoria Park, M14. My thoughts will, in the fullness of time, turn forward again and I will look ahead to working to help others living with Parkinson's.

While I still can I will walk, if not up the hills of the Peak District, then around the base of them as much as possible. I will drive my car up and down the country relishing the challenge. I will write: perhaps articles, perhaps a novel or a thriller and perhaps more poetry and better poetry at that. I will read and I will slow the pace of life so that it does not take the toll on me that I have let it take in recent years. I'll make a point of keeping up with friends by actively staying in contact whilst I can get to them. I recognise that this all sounds perhaps a bit maudlin, a bit negative but it's not. It's realistic.

And so we leap forward to the end of an era. It is October 2013. I have been retired now for two years and the number of things have occurred which bring the story to a happy conclusion. I am not known as a party animal and my original intent was to quietly leave the inspectorate once my retirement and pension details had been resolved. This proved unacceptable to a number of people and I was gently persuaded rather than pressurised to reconsider my position.

For a retirement, a day which I still viewed as my being thrown onto the scrapheap, the Inspectorate will provide and set up an event for the individual to say farewell. The venue will be secured, people notified, food and drink provided and somebody will speak on behalf of the organisation to wish the retiree well for the future. I was really taken by surprise at some of the people who took the trouble to attend. Two of my former Chief Officers, (one of whom had been my line manager so very many years ago in Community Service). Chris Noah, now Deputy Chief Officer of Greater Manchester Probation, erstwhile colleague of Ray Wegrzyn in Salford and with whom I have had more or less parallel career steps, had managed to free up the time, which gave me particular delight. Above all though, the presence of Dot, Matt and Danielle and Richard and Jen was the thing that made this event feel like the significant day it actually was.

Liz, my dear boss for so many years and who had so effectively handled my illness as far as work was concerned was now the Chief Inspector of Probation. This was a much deserved appointment and one which would help take the organisation forward. She had researched my career as well as she could and gave a lovely, entertaining and not too embarrassing talk.

As well as a significant financial collection and a bouquet of flowers for Dot, the team had put together an Inspection report on me; an opportunity for colleagues of all roles and members of inspected bodies to comment on their experience of me. I was stunned by the thought and the effort and floored by the comments.

I was happy enough with that idea but I also wanted family and friends to be involved. So I organised another event to take place at my sister's pub in Manchester later on that same evening. This was a vegetarian spread event with the live music by my saxophone teacher. My sister and her husband took charge of organising the food and did a very splendid job. Everyone thoroughly enjoyed the music and commented on how well it fitted with the general atmosphere in the place that evening. Everybody from the work event was invited to join my family and friends at the pub. I was so pleased to see how many of my colleagues, or now former colleagues I should call them, did come down and join in. It was a good do and I have to say that although it was not something I had been looking forward to I did enjoy the support that I received by everybody taking the trouble to come down for my retirement.

As I sit at my desk on a grey Saturday in October 2013, I realise that I'm coming to another significant point in my life. After just short of 29 years, Dot and I are moving. Next weekend we take possession of a house which is better suited to how we know future needs are likely to shape. It will be a real adventure. We are in the fortunate position of having enough money to buy the house even though we haven't yet sold the one we currently live in. When we do sell this we will have enough money to get all the jobs done, update the bathrooms and especially the kitchen and we will be better placed to live actively through the coming years and to manage the inevitable decline that happens if you live long enough.

Reflecting on the two years since retirement I realise that although not functioning at anything like the level that one has to at work, I have some achievements under my belt of which I can be personally reasonably satisfied.

I took saxophone lessons for two years. An almost lifelong ambition realised so late. I would love to have done better than I have. I found a teacher locally, an excellent saxophonist with a very good, broad approach to the subject and very happy to use any type of music that suited me. As one might imagine, I probably didn't practice enough and there were things missing from the process. However, there was an undoubted success as, by the end of the two years of lessons I can play tunes on the saxophone to my satisfaction if not anybody else's. Translated into work speak that's a goal set and delivered! I would get a bonus on my appraisal!!

It is one of those situations where you realise early on that here is a pastime that can be as expensive as you wish and which comes in with a guaranteed minimum which may well be more than you expected. You buy a cheap instrument at first because you don't know how you will get on. Lessons are likely to cost easily £25 per hour. And then you get told that you have to buy reeds on a fairly regular basis. But first, you need to identify the one that you like/suits you the best. So you need to try a lot of different ones and remember the feel and sound of them as you are learning fingering.

One of the promises made to myself when I went off work was to keep more contact with family and friends. Again this is a well achieved objective. I have certainly kept in better touch with a number of people. It is surprising though, just how much time travelling and visiting can take. So I'm happy to have increased contact with some people and I'll keep working on improving my links with others. One of the things that struck me about these contacts has been the way almost everybody says that they wished that they could do the same and how difficult people found it. This was not surprising to me, given people's work and commitments to immediate family etc. However I have been struck by the appreciation from a few people, openly expressed, for having made this ambition and achieved it to the extent that I have. A couple of people have very plainly said please don't let the fact that I can't get back you often stop you from contacting me. So I don't.

Probably the most significant development or ambition to have achieved has been the establishment of a registered charity. This has been achieved only with the unceasing support of Tom, Debra and Wasyl. Having invited them to be involved, we started to put in place a system of formal planning meetings where we discussed the principal idea and policies in supporting ideas and documentation that would be required to establish a charity that would do what we wanted. What we wanted was an organisation that would raise funds and make grants available, or provide the wherewithal for people with Parkinson's to undertake sports or arts activities.

Over time this developed to include making it possible for people to engage in dance as a form of treatment or therapy. After a lot of work I was able to complete the Charity commission application form and after a few queries from them we were awarded the status of a charitable trust on 13 February 2013. From then until now we continue to meet formally to consider marketing, fundraising etc. The first year is notoriously difficult for small charities and without backup there is a limit to what we can achieve. However we have hung on and learned a considerable amount and I am confident that our second year turnover will be considerably more than the first. We have been learning how to use Facebook and Twitter to link with our website and our Virgin Money Giving homepage, so that as many people as possible get exposed to our existence.

All three of my colleague trustees are working full-time or indeed more than full-time and the gratitude I feel for them and their efforts to fit in something to support my ambition is difficult for me to describe. I know they are there. Friendship is a wonderful yet strange relationship. What makes two people stay in touch with each other for more than 40 years? What makes two people tolerate differences and support agreements actively. Why do two people who live in different parts of the country with families at different stages with totally opposite careers as well as some similar interests want to get together travelling over 100 miles when necessary to support one or other's idea? Why do two people, one of whom had worked for the other a decade previously, wants to rebuild a strong element of that working relationship and develop its embryonic friendship when they don't have to?

I don't know. I do know that having known Wasyl Muszanskyj probably since before infants School, he is without doubt my most long-standing friend and the one with whom I have probably had far and away the most contact, not just by dint of the length of our relationship but by its intensity too. I have known him through thick and thin, through good times and bad, rows and disagreements and pain. He was my first phone call when Conrad died. When Dot's sister tragically died suddenly and far too young, it was Wasyl I met up with later that day just to unload, which I knew I could do with him, openly and honestly. On both of those occasions, he has been a rock. He has dropped everything to be available to me and I know if I need him he will be there. This sounds rather one sided, but I don't think the reality is quite like that. It feels to me and I hope to him as an equitable friendship which does not count the pennies

I met Tom Davenport in the fourth year at grammar school. I was struck by a 15-year-old who took out a pocket watch when I asked him the time. Always brasher than me. Always more physically able than me and for a long time, I always thought him cleverer than me. I now know that we are well matched and I can hold my own in a debate. Tom was a more confident youngster that I was, but I have caught up in some spheres. We were intensely close friends at school along with Stephen, who I still see. After school we went in very different ways and there were some long gaps in our contact. Nevertheless, we kept going and overtime our adult friendship became at least as substantial as it had been in our teenage years.

I have known Debra for about 20 years. She worked in the administrative side of Greater Manchester Probation and provided information and performance data to Salford district where I worked as a young main grade probation officer and then subsequently as the district manager. At this time Deb was the administrative manager for the whole district and one of my team of middle managers. She is a capable, courageous woman who was not as confident in her ability as I was. When I left Salford she maintained contact which I was glad for her to do, as a real friendship grew to overtake a working relationship, which remains the situation for which I am sincerely grateful.

All three have been completely frank in saying that their reason for involvement in the Charity is to support me. I find it hard to be a person considered worthy of supporting and especially so when I am told that I am the story and it's my life and my condition and circumstances which are the features of interest and which need to be used to generate that interest to raise money. I'm getting there. Dot keeps me incredibly well grounded and if there were any chance of me becoming large headed and not fitting through the doorway or if I start to talk about me, me, me, she would soon douse me with a bucket of cold water.

I don't know the answers to the questions I have just asked. I always advise people that, whenever possible, they should know the answer before asking a question. But I don't know these. What I do know though is that I have benefitted hugely from these friendships. Not only practically, but also emotionally and spiritually. I hope that my friends receive half the gain from me that I have from them. This is not to say that there are not other friends and/or relatives. There are, equally important to me and each I hope, having a place for me in their hearts. True friendship is surely one of the things that make the world go round. Cherish it if you find it.

Sometime on, it's 2017. I've been editing this script and doing quite well as far as Parkinson's impact goes. Yes, there is deterioration but it's small steps and slow progress so I keep hopeful that it will last me out. I've not done so well on exercise and weight, so there's room for improvement there. Something that my neurologist once said to me has never left me and I ought to pay more attention to it. I asked him how Parkinson's affected life expectancy. Of course I knew that Parkinson's itself doesn't cause death. He explained very simply; living with Parkinson's takes up your resources so there is nothing left to fight a serious illness such as cancer, pneumonia or a bad infection of some other sort. Despite my history I still to an extent crave the invulnerability of youth. When you know you feel generally okay it's hard to think about getting another illness. Sometimes, my own short-sightedness staggers me.

Chapter 32 – and there's more...

It was 2:30 AM I noticed on the clock on the desk opposite me. I've been here for about 7 ½ hours although still not sure what's happening, except that I need to be here I'm told and there's a small degree of concern quite clearly amongst the medics.

Yes it's a hospital ward. Well a medical assessment unit in fact. I went to see the practice nurse at my GP surgery today. I've been feeling odd for a couple of weeks with symptoms such as sweating profusely, needing to go to the loo a lot and very urgently, dry mouth and drinking a lot of allsorts of non-alcoholic stuff. Amongst other things, the nurse wanted to check my blood sugar levels. Once she got a sample of blood on her machine it failed to register which, she tells me, means that it's far too high. In terms of the numbers (I don't know what the numbers actually mean scientifically speaking) blood sugars should be somewhere between four and seven apparently. If they are too much above or below these parameters it can get quite dodgy, with unconsciousness an option if it's too low and damage to vision or circulation and associated bits if it's too high. Once they saw that mine were clearly too high they told me I needed to come to A & E, and I wasn't to drive myself. So another phone call to patient Matthew (that's patient as in steady and considerate and tolerant) to ask him to come and pick me up and take me to hospital. This all duly happened, me in a slightly confused state and not really very able to function and relying on Dot to throw some things in a bag for me and to tell me what I needed.

We arrived at the hospital and wandered round until we found our way to the A&E reception. I explained the situation and was of course invited to take a seat. The system here, which I guess is the same in most places, is that you're interviewed by a triage nurse fairly quickly and then decisions are made about what should happen. It wasn't too long a wait before I was called in. I explained my symptoms to her and handed over the paperwork that I'd been given at the GP's office. Then it was back out to the waiting room to see what would happen. It was getting late and I was concerned at Dot and Matt waiting much longer as if I was to be admitted then they would be very late getting home and if I was not I could always jump in a taxi to get myself home. After due consideration and deliberation we agreed that they would go and I would be in touch by phone when I had something to say.

Whilst waiting I took the time to phone Richard down in West Sussex. Clearly geography makes it very difficult for him to do anything to help in a situation like this. However his heart is 100% there and he offers to do whatever he can to be helpful. You can tell he is concerned if one of us is unwell and wants to know that we are doing the right things to get fixed. I updated him and told him I'd let him know as well once I had something to say. Eventually I was called through the double doors and shown into a cubicle. I got up on the space age bed and sat, uncomfortably, waiting for something to happen and listening to the world go by on the other side of the curtain. Eventually a young sister put her head through the curtain and checked my identity. She then came in, introduced herself and set about taking a number of routine measurements like blood pressure, oxygen levels and so on. Funnily enough (so I think anyway) due to the odd position I was in, my anxiety being very high and being the focus of attention of people in medical uniforms, I started to display dyskinesia and tremor quite significantly. This in fact to the point that the Blood Pressure Cuff wouldn't take a reading. She wasn't able to measure my blood pressure at all. Eventually, in good humour she gave up. She measured blood sugar as well and this time her machine did get a reading which she said was still very high. More periods of waiting followed with a visit by a doctor who asked a variety of questions, looked at some results and examined me by prodding and poking asking if I had pain. I had no pain at all in fact the only discomfort of the symptoms was the need to urinate frequently and urgently. The sweating was a bit of a nuisance but eminently manageable.

After several more visits interspersed with long sessions of waiting, the doctor came back in the said that I needed to be admitted. I was shocked and very unhappy at the prospect. I asked why in particular I needed to stay when I had been told that once my blood levels came down I would be able to go home. He said that the blood sugar levels were still very high and it wasn't really safe for me to leave, that hospital was the best place to be if anything were to happen as a consequence of the raised levels of sugar. I'm not sufficient of an idiot not to realise that reality of the situation and the sensibleness of his comments. I reluctantly accepted the offer of a bed for the night fully assuming I would be going home in the morning with reduced levels of blood sugar. I notified Dot and the boys accordingly and sat back to wait for some people to come and push the trolley with me on it. Two guys appeared after about 10 minutes, full of the joys and being very warm and pleasant. They trundled the trolley along the corridors and into the lift and then along to the medical assessment unit. As they pushed the trolley onto one of the wards I noted that there were six beds, only one of which was empty and that was the one next to the nursing station. My mind leaped back to tales of the dying being rotated around the ward going nearer to the nursing station the more poorly they got and further away the better they were. Given that there were only six beds and five were occupied I wasn't really overly concerned by the memory, but I have to admit it kept popping into my mind. I clambered off the trolley and onto the bed and sat there listening to the grunts and snores of my five colleagues.

"Oh my God, nurse I've got to piss! Get me something, get me something oh my God!" yelled the man across the room. I felt sorry for him and the nurse, as she hurried to try and accommodate his wishes. Silence settled for a few moments and then I heard a whispering from the bed next to mine: yes... Yes... Yes.... Yes.... I wondered what on earth was going on but didn't want to look and find out. After a while the sister came over to say hello and fill in various admission forms. We chatted off and on while she did that, me supplying the information as requested. She was pleasant and inspired confidence and took various samples of blood and so forth without injuring me unduly!

My background in criminal justice has given me a particular perspective on institutions and institutionalisation. I'm used to prisons, closed institutions wherein prisoners are institutionalised as quickly as possible which helps management of the establishment to run more smoothly. That's a very rough and relatively superficial account. One of its methods is to leave as little as possible to the individual to do at their own wish and to keep as much of the time pre-ordained as possible. Hospital however, whilst still an institution and needing people to cooperate in order for it to run effectively is very much an open institution. People can get on with whatever they are able to get on with and there's a much more individualised approach, which can sometimes verge on you having to work it out for yourself. So I sat for a while longer wondering what I should do. Nobody mentioned anything, or walked over to tell me anything although they did say 'hi' as they passed. After a while I decided since it was the small hours of the morning I would try and sleep a bit although with shouty and whispery I wasn't sure I could get much achieved as far as refreshing sleep went. This was underlined when, an hour or so later, I was woken up to give more blood for blood sugar tests and to have my blood pressure taken.

I remained awake then as it wasn't long before the ward started to come to life. It's interesting to watch this happening. Various people come onto the ward with various purposes. Some are clearly qualified, some not so much. Cups of tea are offered. Lots of blood pressure is checked and presumably other people's blood is taken as well as mine. People get out of bed and wander off to the loo or shout for assistance. The bubble of sound grows gradually bigger, never becoming exactly loud but rising above the hushed murmurs of the middle of the night. People start to arrive for the staff shift change. Handovers happening in groups or pairs, people renewing friendships or being introduced to new colleagues. Details of patients most intimate bodily fluid information being exchanged. People seem to walk a little more purposefully and generally an air of a workplace descends.

I am unsure what to do about food. This is a bad thing. I like food. I don't smoke, I don't drink alcohol and I don't eat flesh or other animal product but I do eat and I eat well. So having to face the prospect of not eating or eating very little which is what I'm picking up is going to be what I have to do to manage this high blood sugar level is quite an unhappy message. Still I'm not daft. I have plenty yet to do so I need to address the problems identified with the help of the medics as best I can. Just the way any of us would do for any funny development in our lives. But on this occasion I actually asked somebody what would make sense for me to have for breakfast in the circumstances. There wasn't a lot of choice. A range of unpleasant breakfast cereals and what they call toast. If I describe this as a square of soggy thin white bread with paste underneath it, you'll perhaps think me unfair and biased. Well yes I am. I like crisp toast with a little bit of butter, preferably made from wholemeal bread. This isn't that by a long, long margin. So I have porridge because I know that's helpful and it's warm and it's there and it's a lot better than the cereals. A jolly woman comes over and filled my water jug gives a clean glass chatting as she goes and offering a cup of tea which is gratefully accepted even though it's not exactly a cup of tea as I would have pretty much anywhere else. Still that's institutions for you.

Measurements of my blood sugar show them still to be too high and I'm injected with insulin and given tablets to take in an attempt to bring them down to somewhere getting near to 10. I am on promise. If my blood sugars get down far enough I can go home. To this end I put a halt on visits on the basis that I expect to get out at any time. My naivete is quite amusing in retrospect. I'm not even allowing for the time it takes for things to change in the body before they can be measured never mind where they start where they finish and what time somebody can actually remember to come and take the measurement. So the day passed oddly with me dozing and being woken by shouty and whispery, who at least now was sitting on the side of his bed doing his whisper yes... Yes... Yes... Apparently in total innocence. There was another chap who cried a lot. He asserted that he was in terrible pain and that nobody was helping him. His crying was rather pathetic and clearly aimed at getting some attention, at which point he stopped crying and started demanding. I don't really know how the nurses deal with people like that. I'd be showing him the door myself. Although I guess they're probably not allowed to do that!!

Blood is taken from one of my fingers on three occasions today and each time the measurements are still reading very high and I am to stay another night. The plan is to pump plenty of insulin and other medications to reduce the blood sugars whilst I sleep so that in the morning they will be nice and normal and I can go home. Oh how I wish for that to happen. It doesn't. The amount of sugar in my blood for some reason stays unfeasibly high and I could see question marks starting to appear on the face of medical staff as their plan has to be reiterated because it hasn't apparently had any of the effects they intended.

The second night has a different team of staff on. It's interesting to see these different groups of people and their managers running the same unit in noticeably different ways. This particular group seemed not so interested in the patients.

I heard more moaning from them than I had the night before or during the day and they enjoyed each other's company perhaps a little more than they should have. I don't want to be too quick to judge because I've little experience of this setting, but that was the impression gained. Anyway I slept better that night, no doubt because of having not slept for a long time prior. I was still awake very early, disturbed by the staff team apparently playing a game of some description. It took a few moments for me to orient myself, but once I remember what was going on I just relaxed and waited for the ward to come alive again. This morning it was an hour later than it had been yesterday which puzzled me that I would have expected that to be a fairly fixed occurrence.

It's a Friday and I'm damned if I'm staying in over the weekend. Conversation with the Doctor is promising in that he sets a new figure for the blood sugars to come down to and talks about the possibility of community, rather than hospital oversight. However even the new numbers are unattainable for my blood sugar which for some reason seems to be clinging to me as if for dear life.

But it is a Friday and nothing much is going to happen over the weekend. If they agree to let me leave I promise I will go to the GP on Monday morning. I don't have to make this argument particularly as one of the doctors takes it upon herself to decide that they will get me home for the weekend and she goes off to discuss her plan of medication with her seniors and the hospital pharmacist. I'm delighted when she comes back to tell me that my blood sugars are down to 18 (or up as high as 18 depending on where you come in from) and that it's fine to me to go home but I must be careful about eating and see the GP early next week. No problem with any of this and to top off my relief at the news, my brother and his wife appeared to visit and were more than happy to give me a lift home, saving me having to call on Matthew to get his old man sorted once again!

Chapter 33 - Conclusion

I have Parkinson's and it will affect me and it will worsen. Like anyone else I don't know what is round the corner in my life but I do know that if I get around the corner Parkinson's will still be there; my shadow, unwanted companion, my nemesis.

I also have diabetes now and am unclear as to how this might affect me in years to come. It's too soon after diagnosis for me to have got my head round the implications of the condition on its own and then I need to factor in the impact of Parkinson's and diabetes one on the other. At the moment all I can figure is that I will need to pay much closer attention to a number of key things in my health otherwise I could easily start to slip down the slope from which there is little prospect of stopping or getting back up. I don't want to be somebody who suffers from complications of something which could have been easily avoided.

It is also realistic for me to determine again, now as I have done several times throughout the course of this quiet adventure, that my life with Parkinson's will be a battle. It will not be a passive, simple takeover by a neurological condition that, certainly at the moment I can say will win eventually. But that winning will come only on the back of heavy resistance from me and those around me. I know already that for somebody who is 23 years post diagnosis I have managed very well by my determination and active engagement with the whole plethora of professionals, as well as by the loving and never-ending support of my family and friends, which let's be honest, makes the whole thing worthwhile. I will continue to respond to their support by engaging with the professionals and by targeting and battling this horrible condition. I will work with like-minded colleagues to raise funds to support PWP who want to improve the quality of their lives. Throughout all of this I will make sure that I do not lose sight of the joys and benefits of my life - with Parkinson's.

Printed in Great Britain
by Amazon

78860484R00139